5

INGREDIENTS

VEGETARIAN

An Hachette UK Company
www.hachette.co.uk

First published in Great Britain in 2015 by Hamlyn,
a division of Octopus Publishing Group Ltd,
Endeavour House,
189 Shaftesbury Avenue,
London,
WC2H 8JY
www.octopusbooks.co.uk

Some of the recipes in this book have previously appeared in other books
published by Hamlyn.

ISBN 978 0 600 62908 5

A CIP catalogue record for this book is available from the British Library.

Printed and bound in China.

10 9 8 7 6 5 4 3 2

Commissioning Editor Eleanor Maxfield
Senior Editor Leanne Bryan
Design Manager Eoghan O'Brien
Designer Jeremy Tilston
Production Controller Sarah Kramer

Standard level spoon measurement are used in all recipes.
1 tablespoon = one 15 ml spoon
1 teaspoon = one 5 ml spoon

Both imperial and metric measurements have been given in all recipes.
Use one set of measurements only and not a mixture of both.

Eggs should be medium unless otherwise stated. The Department of Health
advises that eggs should not be consumed raw. This book contains dishes
made with raw or lightly cooked eggs. It is prudent for more vulnerable people
such as pregnant and nursing mothers, invalids, the elderly, babies and young
children to avoid uncooked or lightly cooked dishes made with eggs. Once
prepared these dishes should be kept refrigerated and used promptly.

Milk should be full-fat unless otherwise stated.

Ovens should be preheated to the specific temperature – if using a fan-assisted
oven, follow manufacturer's instructions for adjusting the time and the temperature.

All microwave information is based on a 650 watt oven. Follow manufacturer's
instructions for an oven with a different wattage.

This book includes dishes made with nuts and nut derivatives. It is advisable for
customers with known allergic reactions to nuts and nut derivatives and those
who may be potentially vulnerable to these allergies, such as pregnant and
nursing mothers, invalids, the elderly, babies and children, to avoid dishes made
with nuts and nut oils. It is also prudent to check the labels of pre-prepared
Ingredients for the possible inclusion of nut derivatives.

JUST 5 INGREDIENTS

VEGETARIAN

MAKE LIFE SIMPLE WITH MORE THAN 100 RECIPES USING 5 INGREDIENTS OR FEWER

hamlyn

CONTENTS

INTRODUCTION

The recipes in this book have been chosen not only for their simplicity and great flavours, but also because they use just five or fewer main ingredients.

Applying a five-ingredient approach to cooking will help you create a repertoire of quick, easily adaptable dishes that are not only cheap and tasty, but also require little shopping and preparation. You will learn to master some basic recipes in record time and learn to appreciate that cooking for yourself is a satisfying and empowering process.

This will make life easier in several ways. As the recipes are straightforward, there is less fiddly preparation. The shopping lists are short and simple – how long do you really want to spend in a supermarket searching for something to cook? The five-ingredient approach is also economical and could help if you are on a budget – you won't be left with half-used packets of ingredients from recipes, which you will never use.

Unlike the other five-ingredient cookbooks out there, the recipes don't use lots of hidden extras. This series requires only 10 additional storecupboard items – easy-to-remember basics that you may already have, but are relatively inexpensive to buy.

Start by stocking up on your storecupboard 10 (see page 11). Make sure you always have at least some of these – that way, you will be just five ingredients away from a decent meal at any time.

Next, choose a recipe that suits the time you have to cook, your energy levels and your mood. Check which of the storecupboard ingredients you will need from the list. The five key ingredients you have to buy to complete the dish are clearly numbered.

One of the best ways to eat cheaply is to avoid buying any costly processed foods. Instead, choose basic ingredients such as vegetables, rice, pasta, fish and chicken, and build your meals around these. You should also try to avoid waste and not spend money on food that has to be thrown away because you run out of time to eat it. Buy food that lasts and plan around the lifetime dates of foods. If you can, freeze the leftovers for another day.

Plan your meals for the week ahead so you only need to go shopping once. When you get into this habit, the ingredients for each meal will be there whenever you need them.

Buy in bulk to get the best prices. Make time to shop around and compare prices in the nearest supermarket, online, your local shops and on market stalls. Stick to buying fruit and vegetables that are in season. Not only will they be better value than exotic produce flown in from abroad, but you will also reduce your food miles. Finally, don't even think about spending precious cash on a supermarket's special offer unless it is something you will actually use. Three tins of pilchards in mustard sauce for the price of one is good value only if you are going to eat them.

Today, you'll find that being a vegetarian, cooking for a vegetarian in your family or choosing to have a couple of meat-free days a week is easy, with supermarkets and health food shops offering ingredients for making tasty and satisfying vegetarian dishes.

Ingredients

For all vegetarians, avoiding certain products can be tricky. For example, animal fat and ingredients such as gelatine may be used in manufactured foods. Rennet, which is extracted from the stomach lining of cows, is often used in cheese making. Also, some jars of curry pastes may contain shrimp. In many cases, there are vegetarian alternatives to these ingredients, so it's advisable to take time to check out food labels.

Cheese

Cheese is a good source of protein for vegetarians, but always check the label to ensure that it is suitable for vegetarians and doesn't contain animal rennet. Some hard cheeses are still made with animal rennet, although increasingly cheese is being made with 'microbial enzymes', widely used in the industry because they are a consistent and inexpensive coagulant.

The term 'microbial enzyme' means that it is a synthetically developed coagulant, while the term 'vegetable rennet' indicates one derived from a vegetable source. Soft cheeses are manufactured without rennet. Some cottage cheeses, however, may contain gelatine, which is derived from animal sources.

The following cheeses are suitable for vegetarians and useful to keep in the fridge: goats' cheese, feta, mozzarella, vegetarian Cheddar, vegetarian pasta cheese (this is a great vegetarian alternative to Parmesan cheese, for use in risottos or pasta dishes), taleggio and ricotta.

Protein

This can come from pulses such as peas, beans and lentils, which are excellent and inexpensive sources of protein and also contain minerals such as iron, zinc and calcium. Soya products, including tofu and QuornTM, contain a form of 'mycoprotein' and are available as mince, burgers, fillets and sausages. Eggs, dairy products, nuts and seeds are also good sources – they contain valuable zinc, calcium and iron, as well as protein.

Iron

Iron is vital for the maintenance of healthy red blood cells and to prevent anaemia. Vegetarian sources include eggs, leafy green vegetables, wholemeal bread, molasses, dried fruit (especially apricots),

pulses, fortified breakfast cereals, peanut butter and pumpkin, sesame and sunflower seeds. Iron from vegetable sources is not as easily absorbed as that from animal sources. If eaten with food rich in vitamin C, the body's absorption of iron is enhanced. Drink fruit juice with breakfast cereal or squeeze fresh lemon juice over green vegetables and salads.

WEEKLY PLANNER

INDULGE YOURSELF

MONDAY
Tomato & feta tart (see page 62)

TUESDAY
Beetroot & goats' cheese crumble (see page 78)

WEDNESDAY
Red rice & pumpkin risotto (see page 156)

THURSDAY
Shallot tart tatin (see page 142)

FRIDAY
Sweet & sour ginger bean curd (see page 158)

SATURDAY
Red onion & goats' cheese tart (see page 134)

STORECUPBOARD 10

The only extras you will need!

1 Sugars
2 Flours
3 Oils & vinegars
4 Baking powder
5 Salt
6 Pepper
7 Stock
8 Onion
9 Garlic
10 Lemon & lemon juice

SHOPPING LIST:

Fruit & vegetables

- 250 g (8 oz) baby plum tomatoes
- 1 kg (2 lb) beetroot
- 750 g (1½ lb) pumpkin
- 500 g (1 lb) shallots

Herbs & spices

- 1 bunch of basil
- ½ teaspoon caraway seeds
- 1 tablespoon lemon thyme
- 1 bunch of thyme
- 300 g (10 oz) fresh root ginger
- small bunch of fresh coriander leaves

Dairy

- 100 g (3½ oz) feta cheese
- 100 g (4 oz) Parmesan cheese
- 115 g (4½ oz) unsalted butter
- 400 g (14 oz) soft round goats' cheese
- 100 ml (3 fl oz) double cream
- 3 eggs

Bottles, tins, cans, packets

- 3 x 320 g (10½ oz) packets ready-rolled puff pastry
- 3 tablespoons pesto
- 250 g (8 oz) Camargue red rice
- 500 g (1 lb) firm bean curd (tofu)
- 2 tablespoons light soy sauce
- 3 tablespoons ready-made tamarind paste (or 2 tablespoons lime juice)
- 175 g (6 oz) plain dark chocolate
- cocoa powder, for dusting

SUNDAY
Rich chocolate mousse (see page 178)

WEEKLY PLANNER

ON A BUDGET

MONDAY
Red pepper soup (see page 34)

TUESDAY
Mushroom stroganoff (see page 82)

WEDNESDAY
Spinach & potato omelette (see page 118)

THURSDAY
Spiced chickpeas with kale (see page 116)

FRIDAY
No-cook-tomato spaghetti (see page 88)

SATURDAY
Caldo verde (see page 38)

STORECUPBOARD 10

The only extras you will need!

1   Sugars
2   Flours
3   Oils & vinegars
4   Baking powder
5   Salt
6   Pepper
7   Stock
8   Onion
9   Garlic
10 Lemon & lemon juice

SUNDAY
Roast tomato & mozzarella salad (see page 56)

SHOPPING LIST:

Fruit & vegetables

- 3 red peppers
- 2 courgettes
- 500 g (1 lb) chestnut mushrooms
- 250 g (8 oz) waxy potatoes such as Charlotte
- 200 g (7 oz) baby spinach leaves
- 100 g (3½ oz) curly kale
- 750 g (1½ lb) very ripe tomatoes
- 125 g (4 oz) dark green cabbage
- 625 g (1½ lb) floury potatoes
- 250 g (8 oz) baby plum tomatoes
- 1 small packet rocket

Herbs & spices

- 1 bunch of chives
- 1 small bunch of parsley
- 1 bunch of basil
- 2 teaspoons fennel seeds
- 1 small bunch of coriander

Dairy

- 1 small pot natural yogurt or double cream
- 15 g (½ oz) butter
- 1 small pot crème fraîche
- 6 large eggs
- 450 g (15 oz) mini mozzarella cheese balls

Bottles, tins, cans, packets

- 1 small jar wholegrain mustard
- 1 small jar mild curry paste
- 400 g (13 oz) can chopped tomatoes
- 400 g (13 oz) can chickpeas
- 400 g (13 oz) dried spaghetti
- 400 g (13 oz) can cannellini beans, drained
- 25 g (1 oz) pine nuts

5 FOR PASTA

Pasta is everybody's favourite comfort food, but it's very easy to fall into the trap of cooking the same old pasta dishes. Use these 5-ingredient recipes as inspiration and to increase your pasta repertoire.

Delicatessen pasta salad (see page 36)

Spaghetti & courgette frittata (see page 64)

Rigatoni with fresh tomato chilli & basil (see page 98)

Basil & rocket pesto with spaghetti (see page 110)

Beetroot pasta with herbs (see page 114)

5 FOR ONE POT

One-pot cooking is the ultimate easy way to cook. Rather than just bunging everything in a casserole and hoping for the best, try out these one-pot recipes to create some fantastic easy meals.

Roasted stuffed peppers (see page 74)

Melanzane parmigiana (see page 90)

Home baked beans (see page 106)

Mushroom & spinach lasagne (see page 138)

Red rice & pumpkin risotto (see page 156)

5 FOR STARTING THE DAY

Get your day off to the brightest start with these delicious 5-ingredients vegetarian breakfast or brunch recipes. Whether it be something savoury or sweet that you fancy, this selection will hit the spot.

Pesto scrambled eggs (see page 66)

Sweetcorn & pepper frittata (see page 84)

Potato rosti with frazzled eggs (see page 92)

Home baked beans (see page 106)

Griddled bananas with blueberries (see page 182)

5 FOR POTATOES

Are you bored of always eating potatoes as an accompaniment to your vegetarian meal? Try these different potato recipes to change it up a little and make potatoes the focus, instead of the side dish, of your recipe.

New potato, basil & pine nut salad (see page 30)

Pea, potato & rocket soup (see page 40)

Spicy apple & potato soup (see page 46)

Asparagus & new potato tortilla (see page 70)

Baked sweet potatoes (see page 126)

5 FOR COOLING DOWN

These 5 summer-inspired recipes will have you thinking of sunshine, blue skies and warm weather in no time. Cook them on a cold winter's day to bring a bit of summer into your life anytime of the year.

Summer green pea soup (see page 26)

Beetroot & orange salad (see page 44)

Broad bean & lemon spaghetti (see page 128)

Melon, ginger & lime sorbet (see page 166)

Summer berry sorbet (see page 168)

5 FOR A PICNIC

Always on the search for a great portable snack? These 5 picnic or lunchbox recipes will be a great source of inspiration. Make a couple of portions so that you have enough to last you through the week.

Bean, lemon & rosemary hummus (see page 104)

Tabbouleh with fruit & nuts (see page 108)

Spinach & potato omelette (see page 118)

Cold Asian summer soba noodle salad (see page 146)

Wild rice & goats' cheese salad (see page 148)

SOUPS & SALADS

SERVES 6

Preparation time 10 minutes
Cooking time 1 hour 5 minutes

INGREDIENTS

1 4 carrots, chopped

2 2 parsnips, chopped

3 1 leek, finely chopped

4 2 teaspoons thyme leaves

5 thyme sprigs, to garnish

STORE CUPBOARD

olive oil, for spraying; 1.2 litres (2 pints) vegetable stock; salt and black pepper

Roast Root Vegetable Soup

■ Place the carrots and parsnips in a roasting tin, spray lightly with olive oil and season with salt and pepper. Roast in a preheated oven, 200°C (400°F), Gas Mark 6, for 1 hour or until the vegetables are soft.

■ Meanwhile, 20 minutes before the vegetables have finished roasting, put the leek in a large saucepan with the stock and 1 teaspoon of the thyme. Cover the pan and simmer for 20 minutes.

■ Transfer the roasted root vegetables to a blender or food processor and blend, adding a little of the stock if necessary. Transfer to the stock saucepan and season to taste. Add the remaining thyme, stir and simmer for 5 minutes to reheat.

■ Ladle into individual bowls and serve garnished with the thyme sprigs.

SERVES 6

Preparation time 25 minutes
Cooking time 20 minutes

INGREDIENTS

1   750 g (1½ lb) large tomatoes on the vine

2   1 baking potato, about 200 g (7 oz), diced

3   1 tablespoon tomato purée

4   small bunch of basil

STORE CUPBOARD

2 tablespoons olive oil; 1 onion, roughly chopped;
2 garlic cloves, finely chopped; 750 ml (1¼ pints)
vegetable or chicken stock; 1 tablespoon soft
brown sugar; 4 teaspoons balsamic vinegar;
salt and black pepper

Tomato & Balsamic Vinegar Soup

■ Cut the tomatoes in half, place them cut-side down in a foil-lined grill pan and drizzle with some oil. Grill for 4–5 minutes until the skins have split and blackened.

■ Meanwhile, fry the onion, potato and garlic in the remaining oil for 5 minutes, stirring occasionally until softened and turning golden around the edges.

■ Peel and roughly chop the tomatoes and add to the onion and potato with the pan juices, then stir in the stock, tomato purée, soft brown sugar and balsamic vinegar. Add half the basil, season and bring to the boil. Cover and simmer for 15 minutes.

■ Purée half the soup in batches in a blender or food processor until smooth. Return to the saucepan with the rest of the soup and reheat. Season to taste, then ladle into bowls, garnish with the remaining basil leaves and serve with Parmesan twists or cheese straws, if liked.

SERVES 4

Preparation time 10 minutes or longer if shelling
fresh peas
Cooking time about 3 minutes

INGREDIENTS

1	1 tablespoon butter
2	1.5 kg (3½ lb) fresh peas, shelled, or 500 g (1 lb) frozen peas
3	2 tablespoons thick natural yogurt or single cream
4	nutmeg
5	1 tablespoon chopped and 2 whole chives, to garnish

STORE CUPBOARD

½ onion, chopped; 750 ml (1¼ pints) vegetable stock

Summer Green Pea Soup

■ Melt the butter in a large pan and soften the onion, but do not allow it to colour. Add the peas to the pan with the stock. Bring to the boil and simmer for around 3 minutes for frozen peas and 2–3 minutes for fresh peas, until they are cooked. Be careful not to overcook fresh peas or they will lose their flavour.

■ Remove from the heat and purée in a blender or food processor. Grate in a little nutmeg. Reheat gently if necessary, and serve with a swirl of yogurt or cream and the chopped and whole chives.

ADD BROAD BEANS & MINT

For minted pea and broad bean soup, fry the onion in the butter as in the main recipe, then add 625 g (1¼ lb) fresh peas and 625 g (1¼ lb) fresh broad beans, both podded or 250 g (8 oz) frozen peas and 250 g (8 oz) frozen broad beans, 2 stems of fresh mint and the stock. Simmer as in the main recipe then purée, reheat and ladle into bowls. Top with 4 tablespoons double cream swirled into the soup and a few tiny fresh mint leaves.

SERVES 4

Preparation time 10 minutes
Cooking time 20 minutes

INGREDIENTS

1 2 celery sticks, thinly sliced

2 2 × 400 g (13 oz) cans butter beans, rinsed and drained

3 4 tablespoons sun-dried tomato paste

4 1 tablespoon chopped rosemary or thyme, plus extra sprigs to decorate

5 Parmesan cheese shavings, to serve

STORE CUPBOARD

3 tablespoons olive oil; 1 onion, finely chopped; 2 garlic cloves, thinly sliced; 900 ml (1½ pints) vegetable stock; salt and black pepper

Butter Bean & Tomato Soup

■ Heat the oil in a saucepan. Add the onion and fry for 3 minutes until softened. Add the celery and garlic and fry for about 2 minutes.

■ Add the butter beans, sun-dried tomato paste, stock, rosemary or thyme and a little salt and pepper. Bring to the boil, then reduce the heat, cover and simmer gently for 15 minutes. Serve sprinkled with the Parmesan shavings and some rosemary or thyme sprigs to garnish.

SERVES 4–6

Preparation time 5 minutes, plus cooling
Cooking time 15 minutes

INGREDIENTS

1   **1 kg (2 lb) new potatoes, scrubbed**

2   **50 g (2 oz) pine nuts, toasted**

3   **½ bunch of basil leaves**

STORE CUPBOARD

4 tablespoons extra virgin olive oil; 1½ tablespoons
white wine vinegar; salt and black pepper

New Potato, Basil & Pine Nut Salad

■ Put the potatoes in a large saucepan
of lightly salted water and bring to the
boil. Cook for 12–15 minutes until tender.
Drain well and transfer to a large bowl.

■ Cut any large potatoes in half.

■ Whisk the oil, vinegar and a little salt
and pepper together in a small bowl.
Add half to the potatoes, stir well and
leave to cool completely.

■ Add the pine nuts, the remaining
dressing and basil, stir well and serve.

MAKE IT TRADITIONAL

For a classic potato salad, cook
1 kg (2 lb) new potatoes as in the
main recipe, drain and leave to cool.
Combine 150 ml (¼ pint) good-
quality mayonnaise with 1 bunch
of finely chopped spring onions,
2 tablespoons chopped fresh chives,
a squeeze of lemon juice and salt
and pepper. Toss with the potatoes.

SERVES 4

Preparation time 20 minutes
Cooking time 30 minutes

INGREDIENTS

1 250 g (8 oz) fennel bulb, thinly sliced

2 1 potato, diced

3 4 tablespoons chopped parsley

4 16 black Greek olives, pitted and chopped

STORE CUPBOARD

6 tablespoons extra-virgin olive oil, plus extra for drizzling; 1 onion, chopped; finely grated rind of 2 lemons, plus juice of 1 lemon; 900 ml (1½ pints) vegetable stock; 1 small garlic clove, finely chopped; salt and black pepper

Fennel Soup with Black Olive Gremolata

■ Heat the oil in a large saucepan, add the onion and cook for 5–10 minutes or until beginning to soften. Add the fennel, potato and rind of 1 lemon and cook for 5 minutes until the fennel begins to soften. Pour in the stock and bring to the boil. Reduce the heat, cover the pan and simmer for about 15 minutes or until the vegetables are tender.

■ Meanwhile, to make the gremolata, mix together the garlic, the remaining lemon rind and the parsley, then stir the chopped olives into the herb mixture. Cover and chill.

■ Blend the soup in a blender or food processor and pass it through a strainer to remove any strings of fennel. The soup should not be too thick, so add more stock if necessary. Return it to the rinsed pan. Taste and season well with salt, pepper and plenty of lemon juice. Pour into warmed bowls and sprinkle each serving with gremolata, to be stirred in before eating, and a drizzle of olive oil. Serve with slices of toasted crusty bread, if you like.

AN ITALIAN CLASSIC

For green olive and thyme gremolata,
mix together 1 finely chopped garlic
clove, finely grated rind of 1 lemon,
4 tablespoons chopped parsley and
2 teaspoons chopped lemon thyme,
then stir in 16 pitted and chopped
green olives. Serve on the soup,
cooked as in the main recipe, and
drizzle with lemon-infused olive oil.

SERVES 4

Preparation time 15 minutes
Cooking time 35 minutes

INGREDIENTS

1   **3 red peppers, deseeded and roughly chopped**

2   **2 courgettes, finely chopped**

3   **natural yogurt or double cream**

4   **chopped chives**

STORE CUPBOARD

2 onions, finely chopped; 2 tablespoons olive oil; 1 garlic clove, crushed ; 900 ml (1½ pints) vegetable stock; salt and black pepper

Red Pepper Soup

■ Put the onions in a large saucepan with the oil and gently fry for 5 minutes or until softened and golden brown. Add the garlic and cook gently for 1 minute.

■ Add the red peppers and half the courgettes and fry for 5–8 minutes or until softened and brown.

■ Add the stock to the pan with salt and pepper and bring to the boil. Reduce the heat, cover the pan and simmer gently for 20 minutes.

■ When the vegetables are tender, blend the mixture in batches in a blender or food processor to a smooth soup and return to the pan.

■ Season to taste, reheat and serve topped with the remaining chopped courgette and garnished with yogurt or a swirl of cream and chopped chives. This vibrant and warming soup is ideal for any meal and tastes just as good warm or cold.

INGREDIENTS

1	2 × 300 g (10 oz) packs fresh spinach and ricotta tortellini
2	1 × 275 g (9 oz) jar mixed sliced roasted peppers in olive oil
3	1 × 275 g (9 oz) jar mushrooms in olive oil, drained
4	200 g (7 oz) sun-blush tomatoes, drained
5	100 g (4 oz) mixed baby leaf and herb salad

STORECUPBOARD

black pepper

Delicatessen Pasta Salad

■ Bring a large pan of lightly salted water to the boil. Add the tortellini and cook according to the pack instructions. Drain well and tip into a large bowl.

■ Add the jar of mixed peppers, including the oil, along with the drained mushrooms and sun-blush tomatoes.

■ Add the baby leaf salad. Season with black pepper, stir gently to combine and serve warm.

Preparation time 15 minutes
Cooking time 35 minutes

INGREDIENTS

1   125 g (4 oz) dark green cabbage, e.g. Cavolo Nero

2   625 g (1½ lb) floury potatoes, cut into small chunks

3   400 g (13 oz) can cannellini beans, drained

4   15 g (½ oz) fresh coriander, roughly chopped

STORE CUPBOARD

4 tablespoons olive oil; 1 large onion, chopped; 2 garlic cloves, chopped; 1 litre (1¾ pints) vegetable stock; salt and black pepper

Caldo Verde

■ Discard any tough stalk ends from the cabbage and roll the leaves up tightly. Using a large knife, shred the cabbage as finely as possible.

■ Heat the oil in a large saucepan and gently fry the onion for 5 minutes. Add the potatoes and cook, stirring occasionally, for 10 minutes. Stir in the garlic and cook for a further 1 minute.

■ Add the stock and bring to the boil. Reduce the heat and simmer gently, covered, for about 10 minutes until the potatoes are tender. Use a potato masher to lightly mash the potatoes into the soup so that they are broken up but not completely puréed.

■ Stir in the beans, cabbage and coriander and cook gently for a further 10 minutes. Season to taste with salt and pepper.

AN IRISH FAVOURITE

For colcannon, boil 500 g (l lb) unpeeled potatoes until tender. Drain and add 150 ml (¼ pint) milk. Meanwhile, boil 500 g (1 lb) finely shredded green cabbage for 10 minutes or until the cabbage is tender. Drain and add 6 finely chopped spring onions. When cool enough to handle, peel and mash the potatoes in a bowl, then beat in the cabbage and spring onions. Season and beat in 50 g (2 oz) butter.

Preparation time 15 minutes
Cooking time 35 minutes

INGREDIENTS

1   2 teaspoons chopped thyme

2   250 g (8 oz) potatoes, chopped

3   500 g (1 lb) frozen or fresh shelled peas

4   100 g (3½ oz) rocket leaves, roughly chopped

STORE CUPBOARD

3 tablespoons extra virgin olive oil, plus extra to serve; 1 onion, finely chopped; 2 garlic cloves, finely chopped; 1 litre (1¾ pints) vegetable stock; juice of 1 lemon; salt and black pepper

Pea, Potato & Rocket Soup

■ Heat the oil in a saucepan, add the onion, garlic and thyme and cook over a low heat, stirring frequently, for 5 minutes until the onion is softened. Add the potatoes and cook, stirring frequently, for 5 minutes.

■ Stir in the peas, stock and salt and pepper. Bring to the boil, then reduce the heat, cover and simmer gently for 20 minutes.

■ Transfer the soup to a blender or food processor, add the rocket and lemon juice and process until smooth. Return to the pan, adjust the seasoning and heat through. Serve immediately, drizzled with a little extra oil.

TRY IT WITH ASPARAGUS

For summer pea and asparagus soup, omit the potatoes and add 250 g (8 oz) asparagus spears. Trim off the tips and cook them in the stock for 3–5 minutes, until tender. Drain and set aside, reserving the stock. Slice the remaining asparagus and add to the soup with the peas. Serve garnished with the tips.

SERVES 4

Preparation time 15 minutes
Cooking time 1¼ hours

INGREDIENTS

1 1 butternut squash

2 a few rosemary sprigs, plus extra to garnish

3 150 g (5 oz) red lentils, washed

STORE CUPBOARD

2 tablespoons olive oil; 1 onion, finely chopped; 900 ml (1½ pints) vegetable stock; salt and black pepper

Butternut Squash & Rosemary Soup

■ Cut the squash in half and use a spoon to scoop out the seeds and fibrous flesh. Peel and cut the squash into small chunks and place in a roasting tin. Sprinkle over the oil and rosemary, and season well with salt and pepper. Roast in a preheated oven, 200°C (400°F), Gas Mark 6, for 45 minutes.

■ Meanwhile, place the lentils in a saucepan, cover with water, bring to the boil and boil rapidly for 10 minutes. Strain, then return the lentils to a clean saucepan with the onion and stock and simmer for 5 minutes. Season to taste.

■ Remove the squash from the oven, mash the flesh with a fork and add to the soup. Simmer for 25 minutes and then ladle into bowls. Garnish with more rosemary before serving.

SERVES 2–4

Preparation time 15 minutes
Cooking time 30 minutes

INGREDIENTS

1	7 small beetroot
2	2 oranges
3	1 teaspoon wholegrain mustard
4	65 g (2½ oz) watercress
5	75 g (3 oz) soft goats' cheese

STORE CUPBOARD

1 tablespoon red wine vinegar; 1½ tablespoons white wine vinegar; 3 tablespoons olive oil; salt and black pepper

Beetroot & Orange Salad

■ Scrub and trim the beetroot and put them in a foil-lined roasting tin with the red wine vinegar and bake in a preheated oven, 190°C (375°F), Gas Mark 5, for 30 minutes or until cooked. Check by piercing one with a knife. Allow the beetroot to cool slightly and then, wearing food-handling gloves, rub off the skin and slice the globes into halves, or quarters if large.

■ Meanwhile, peel and segment the oranges. Make the dressing by whisking the white wine vinegar, oil and mustard together. Season with salt and pepper.

■ Put the watercress in a bowl with the beetroot and add the dressing. Mix gently to combine. Arrange the oranges on a plate, top with the beetroot and watercress and crumble over the cheese. Season with black pepper and serve.

Preparation time 15 minutes
Cooking time 30 minutes

INGREDIENTS

| **1** | 65 g (2½ oz) butter |

| **2** | 2 dessert apples, peeled, cored and sliced, plus ½–1 dessert apple, peeled, cored and diced, to garnish |

| **3** | pinch of cayenne pepper (or to taste), plus extra for sprinking |

| **4** | 300 g (10 oz) floury potatoes, sliced |

| **5** | 300 ml (½ pint) hot milk |

STORE CUPBOARD

1 small onion, chopped; 600 ml (1 pint) vegetable stock; salt

Spicy Apple & Potato Soup

■ Melt 50 g (2 oz) of the butter in a large heavy-based saucepan over a medium heat. Add the onion and cook for 5 minutes or until softened. Add the 2 sliced apples and cayenne and cook, stirring, for another 2 minutes.

■ Pour in the stock, then add the potatoes. Bring to the boil, then reduce the heat and simmer gently for 15–18 minutes until the apples and potatoes are very tender.

■ Blend the soup in batches in a blender or food processor until very smooth, then transfer to a clean saucepan. Reheat gently and stir in the hot milk. Taste and adjust the seasoning if necessary.

■ Meanwhile, make the apple garnish. Melt the remaining butter in a small frying pan, add the diced apple and cook over a high heat until crisp.

■ Serve the soup in warm bowls, garnishing each portion with some diced apple and a sprinkling of cayenne.

Preparation time 20 minutes
Cooking time 25 minutes

INGREDIENTS

1   **500 g (1 lb) pumpkin**

2   **2 thyme sprigs, roughly chopped**

3   **200 g (7 oz) mixed baby salad leaves**

4   **50 g (2 oz) feta cheese**

5   **2 tablespoons toasted pine nuts,
to garnish**

STORE CUPBOARD

2 tablespoons balsamic vinegar; 4 tablespoons
olive oil, plus extra for drizzling; salt and
black pepper

Pumpkin, Feta & Pine Nut Salad

■ Skin and deseed the pumpkin, cut the
flesh into 2 cm (¾ inch) squares and put
them in a roasting tin. Drizzle with olive oil,
scatter over the thyme and season with
salt and pepper. Roast the pumpkin in a
preheated oven, 190°C (375°F), Gas Mark
5, for 25 minutes or until cooked though.
Remove the pumpkin from the oven and
allow to cool slightly.

■ Meanwhile, make the dressing. Whisk
together the vinegar and 4 tablespoons
of oil and set aside.

■ Put the mixed leaves in a large
salad bowl, add the cooked pumpkin
and crumble in the feta. Drizzle over the
dressing and toss carefully to combine.
Transfer the mixture to serving plates,
garnish with toasted pine nuts and
serve immediately.

Preparation time 15 minutes
Cooking time 20 minutes

INGREDIENTS

1 375 g (12 oz) leeks, slit and well washed then thinly sliced

2 375 g (12 oz) fresh shelled or frozen peas

3 small bunch mint, plus a few leaves to garnish (optional)

4 150 g (5 oz) full-fat mascarpone cheese

STORE CUPBOARD

2 tablespoons olive oil; 900 ml (1½ pints) vegetable stock; grated rind of 1 small lemon, plus lemon rind curls to garnish (optional); salt and black pepper

Cream of Leek & Pea Soup

■ Heat the oil in a saucepan, add the leeks, toss in the oil, then cover and fry gently for 10 minutes, stirring occasionally, until softened but not coloured. Mix in the peas and cook briefly.

■ Pour the stock into the pan, add a little salt and pepper, then bring to the boil. Cover and simmer gently for 10 minutes.

■ Ladle half the soup into a blender or food processor, add all the mint and blend until smooth. Pour the purée back into the saucepan. Mix the mascarpone with half of the lemon rind, reserving the rest to be used as a garnish.

■ Spoon half the mascarpone mixture into the soup, then reheat, stirring until the mascarpone has melted. Taste and adjust the seasoning if needed. Ladle the soup into bowls, top with spoonfuls of the remaining mascarpone and a sprinkling of the remaining lemon rind. Garnish with mint leaves and lemon rind curls, if liked.

ADD WATERCRESS

For cream of leek, pea and
watercress soup, use just 175 g
(6 oz) peas and add a roughly
chopped bunch of watercress.
Simmer in 600 ml (1 pint) of
stock, then instead of adding the
mascarpone, stir in 150 ml (¼ pint)
milk and 150 ml (¼ pint) double
cream, drizzling a little extra cream
over at the end and topping with
some crispy grilled and chopped
bacon to garnish.

Preparation time 15 minutes, plus resting
Cooking time 12 minutes

INGREDIENTS

1   250 g (8 oz) malloreddus or orzo pasta

2   250 g (8 oz) frozen peas, thawed

3   6 spring onions, roughly chopped

4   8 marinated artichoke hearts, thinly sliced

5   4 tablespoons chopped mint

STORE CUPBOARD

6 tablespoons olive oil; 2 garlic cloves, crushed;
rind and juice of ½ lemon, plus grated lemon rind
to garnish; salt and black pepper

Warm Pasta Salad

■ Cook the pasta in a saucepan of lightly
salted boiling water for about 6 minutes
or according to the instructions on the
packet. Add the thawed peas and cook for
a further 2–3 minutes until the peas and
pasta are cooked. Drain well.

■ Meanwhile, heat 2 tablespoons of oil in
a frying pan and stir-fry the spring onions
and garlic for 1–2 minutes until softened.

■ Stir the spring onions and garlic into
the pasta with the artichokes, mint and
the remaining oil. Toss well, season with
salt and pepper, then leave to rest for
10 minutes. Stir in the lemon juice and serve
the salad warm, garnished with lemon rind.

SERVES 6

Preparation time 20 minutes
Cooking time 1–1¼ hours

INGREDIENTS

1	750 g (1½ lb) carrots, diced

2	40 g (1½ oz) long-grain rice

3	300 ml (½ pint) milk

4	15 g (½ oz) fresh mint, plus leaves to garnish (optional)

STORE CUPBOARD

5 tablespoons olive oil; 1 onion, roughly chopped; 1 litre (1¾ pints) vegetable stock; ¼ teaspoon caster sugar; salt and black pepper

Smooth Carrot Soup with Mint Oil

■ Heat 2 tablespoons of the oil in a pan, add the onion and fry for 5 minutes until just beginning to soften and turn golden around the edges. Stir in the carrots and cook for 5 minutes. Mix in the rice, stock and a little salt and pepper. Bring to the boil, then cover and simmer for 45 minutes, stirring occasionally until the carrots are cooked and tender.

■ Meanwhile, make the mint oil. Strip the leaves from the mint stems and add the leaves to a blender or food processor with the sugar and a little pepper. Finely chop, then gradually blend in the remaining oil a little at a time with the motor running. Spoon into a small bowl and stir before using.

■ Rinse the blender or food processor, then purée the soup in batches until smooth. Return the soup to the saucepan and stir in the milk. Reheat, then taste and adjust the seasoning if needed. Ladle into bowls then drizzle with the mint oil and add some extra mint leaves if liked. Serve with muffins (see opposite) if liked.

MAKE SAVOURY MUFFINS

For courgette muffins, put 300 g (10 oz) self-raising flour into a bowl, and add 3 teaspoons baking powder, 75 g (3 oz) freshly grated Parmesan cheese, 200 g (7 oz) coarsely grated courgette, 150 ml (5 oz) low-fat natural yogurt, 3 tablespoons olive oil, 3 eggs and 3 tablespoons milk. Fork together until just mixed, and divide into a 12 hole muffin tin lined with paper cases. Bake in a preheated oven, 200°C (400°F), Gas Mark 6, for 18–20 minutes until well risen and golden brown. Serve warm.

INGREDIENTS

1 250 g (8 oz) baby plum or cherry tomatoes, halved

2 25 g (1 oz) rocket leaves

3 12 basil leaves

4 150 g (5 oz) mini mozzarella balls, drained

5 25 g (1 oz) pine nuts, toasted

STORE CUPBOARD

1 tablespoon olive oil; 4 tablespoons extra virgin olive oil; 1 teaspoon red wine vinegar; salt and black pepper

Roast Tomato & Mozzarella Salad

■ Place the tomatoes, cut-side up, in a small roasting tin. Drizzle over 1 tablespoon of olive oil and season with a little sea salt and pepper. Roast in a preheated oven, 200°C (400°F), Gas Mark 6, for 20 minutes until wilted and softened. Remove from the oven and leave to cool.

■ Make the dressing. Place the rocket and basil leaves, 2 tablespoons of the extra virgin olive oil and the vinegar in a small bowl. Blend with a stick blender to a purée, or transfer to a mini food processor to blend. Stir in the remaining oil and season to taste with salt and pepper.

■ Arrange the roasted tomatoes on a platter, then tear the mozzarella balls in half and arrange among the tomatoes. Drizzle over the dressing and scatter over the pine nuts. Serve immediately.

CREATE A DRESSING

For basil dressing to serve as an alternative dressing for the salad, use 20 g (¾ oz) basil leaves in place of the rocket and basil and follow the main recipe. Serve the salad with a handful of rocket leaves.

SERVES 6

Preparation time 15 minutes, plus soaking
Cooking time 30 minutes

INGREDIENTS

1 30 g (1½ oz) parsley

2 410 g (13½ oz) can chickpeas, drained
and rinsed

STORE CUPBOARD

1 small onion; 3 garlic cloves; 2 tablespoons olive
oil; 1.2 litres (2 pints) vegetable stock; grated rind
and juice of ½ lemon; salt and black pepper

Chickpea & Parsley Soup

■ Put the onion, garlic and parsley in a
food processor or blender and process
until finely chopped.

■ Heat the oil in a saucepan and cook the
onion mixture over a low heat until slightly
softened. Add the chickpeas and cook
gently for 1–2 minutes.

■ Add the stock, season well with salt and
pepper and bring to the boil. Cover and
cook for 20 minutes or until the chickpeas
are really tender. Allow the soup to cool
for a while, then partly purée it in a food
processor or blender or mash it with a fork
so that it retains plenty of texture.

■ Pour the soup into a clean pan, add
the lemon juice and adjust the seasoning
if necessary. Heat through gently. Serve the
soup topped with grated lemon rind and
black pepper.

TRY IT WITH BEANS

For flageolet, cannellini and parsley soup, replace the chickpeas with 200 g (7 oz) each canned flageolet and cannellini beans, and use the rind and juice of 1 lemon. Otherwise, cook as in the main recipe.

MIDWEEK MEALS

SERVES 4

Preparation time 15 minutes
Cooking time 20 minutes

INGREDIENTS

1 | 350 g (11½ oz) puff pastry, defrosted if frozen

2 | 3 tablespoons pesto

3 | 250 g (8 oz) baby plum tomatoes, halved

4 | 100 g (3½ oz) feta cheese, crumbled

5 | handful of basil leaves

STORE CUPBOARD

plain flour, for dusting; salt and black pepper

Tomato & Feta Tart

■ Roll the pastry out on a lightly floured work surface to form a 25 × 35 cm (10 × 14 inches) rectangle. Using a sharp knife, score a 2.5 cm (1 inch) border around the edges. Transfer to a baking sheet and spread the pesto over the pastry.

■ Arrange the tomatoes and feta over the top. Season with salt and pepper. Bake in a preheated oven, 220°C (425°F), Gas Mark 7, for 20 minutes until the pastry is puffed and golden. Remove from the oven and scatter over the basil leaves.

Preparation time 10 minutes
Cooking time 25 minutes

INGREDIENTS

1	2 courgettes, thinly sliced
2	4 eggs
3	125 g (4 oz) cooked spaghetti
4	4 tablespoons freshly grated Parmesan cheese
5	10 basil leaves

STORE CUPBOARD

2 tablespoons olive oil; 1 onion, thinly sliced; 1 garlic clove, crushed; salt and black pepper

Spaghetti & Courgette Frittata

■ Heat the oil in a heavy-based, ovenproof, nonstick 23 cm (9 inch) frying pan over a low heat. Add the onion and cook, stirring occasionally, for 6–8 minutes until softened. Stir in the courgettes and garlic and cook, stirring, for 2 minutes.

■ Beat the eggs in a large bowl and season with salt and pepper. Stir in the cooked courgettes and garlic, spaghetti and half the Parmesan and basil. Pour the mixture into the frying pan and quickly arrange the ingredients so they are evenly dispersed. Cook over a low heat for 8–10 minutes, or until all but the top of the frittata is set.

■ Transfer to a preheated very hot grill and place about 10 cm (4 inches) from the heat source. Cook until set but not coloured.

■ Give the pan a shake to loosen the frittata, then transfer to a plate. Scatter the top with the remaining Parmesan and basil and leave to cool for 5 minutes before serving.

SERVES 4

Preparation time 5 minutes
Cooking time 5 minutes

INGREDIENTS

1   **12 eggs**

2   **100 ml (3½ fl oz) single cream**

3   **25 g (1 oz) butter**

4   **4 slices of granary bread, toasted**

5   **4 tablespoons pesto**

STORE CUPBOARD

salt and black pepper

Pesto Scrambled Eggs

■ Beat the eggs, cream and a little salt and pepper together in a bowl. Melt the butter in a large, nonstick frying pan, add the egg mixture and stir over a low heat with a wooden spoon until cooked to your liking.

■ Put a slice of toast on each serving plate. Spoon a quarter of the scrambled eggs on to each slice of toast, make a small indent in the centre and add a tablespoonful of pesto. Serve immediately.

MAKE IT CHEESY

For cheesy scrambled eggs, stir
125 g (4 oz) diced soft goats'
cheese and 2 tablespoons chopped
parsley into the eggs just before
serving, and omit the pesto.

Preparation time 10 minutes
Cooking time about 25 minutes

INGREDIENTS

1	2 aubergines, sliced in half lengthways
2	250 g (8 oz) can chopped tomatoes
3	1 tablespoon tomato purée
4	300 g (10 oz) mozzarella cheese, cut into 8 thin slices
5	basil leaves, to garnish

STORE CUPBOARD

3 tablespoons olive oil; 1 onion, chopped; 1 garlic clove, crushed; salt and black pepper

Baked Aubergines & Mozzarella

■ Brush the aubergines with 2 tablespoons of the oil and arrange, cut-side up, on a baking sheet. Roast in a preheated oven, 200°C (400°F), Gas Mark 6, for 20 minutes.

■ Meanwhile, heat the remaining oil in a frying pan, add the onion and garlic and cook until the onion is soft and starting to brown. Add the tomatoes and tomato purée and simmer for 5 minutes or until the sauce has thickened.

■ Remove the aubergines from the oven and cover each half with some sauce and 2 of the mozzarella slices. Season to taste with salt and pepper and return to the oven for 4–5 minutes to melt the cheese. Serve immediately scattered with basil leaves.

SERVES 4

Preparation time 15 minutes
Cooking time 40 minutes

INGREDIENTS

1   350 g (11½ oz) asparagus spears

2   400 g (13 oz) new potatoes

3   6 eggs

4   5 g (¼ oz) basil leaves, torn into pieces

STORE CUPBOARD

100 ml (3½ fl oz) olive oil; 1 onion, chopped;
salt and black pepper

Asparagus & New Potato Tortilla

■ Snap the woody ends off the asparagus and cut the spears into 5 cm (2 inch) lengths. Slice the potatoes very thinly.

■ Heat 50 ml (2 fl oz) of the oil in a sturdy frying pan about 25 cm (10 inches) across. Add the asparagus and fry gently for 5 minutes until slightly softened. Lift out with a slotted spoon on to a plate. Add the remaining oil to the pan and scatter in the potatoes and onion. Cook very gently, turning frequently in the oil, for about 15 minutes until the potatoes are tender.

■ Beat the eggs with a little salt and pepper in a bowl and stir in the basil leaves. Add the asparagus to the pan and combine the vegetables so that they are fairly evenly distributed. Pour the egg mixture over the vegetables and reduce the heat to its lowest setting. Cover with a lid or foil and cook for about 10 minutes until almost set but still a little wobbly in the centre.

■ Loosen the edge of the tortilla, cover the pan with a plate and invert the tortilla on to it. Slide back into the pan and return to the heat for 2–3 minutes until the base has firmed up. Slide on to a clean plate and serve warm or cold, cut into wedges, with Hollandaise sauce (see opposite) if liked.

A CLASSIC SAUCE

For hollandaise sauce, put
1 tablespoon white wine vinegar
in a food processor with 2 egg
yolks. Blend lightly to combine.
Cut 150 g (5 oz) butter into
pieces and melt gently in a small
saucepan. Pour into a jug. With the
machine running, very slowly pour
in the melted butter until thick and
smooth. Season to taste with salt
and pepper and add a dash of hot
water if the sauce is very thick.
Spoon over the tortilla, if liked.

Preparation time 15 minutes
Cooking time 10–12 minutes

INGREDIENTS

1	200 g (7 oz) dried penne or other pasta shapes
2	200 g (7 oz) shelled broad beans, fresh or frozen
3	50 g (2 oz) sun-blush tomatoes in oil, drained and roughly chopped
4	handful of mixed herbs, such as parsley, tarragon, chervil and chives, roughly chopped
5	50 g (2 oz) feta cheese, crumbled or roughly chopped

STORE CUPBOARD

2 tablespoons extra virgin olive oil; 1 tablespoon sherry vinegar; ½ garlic clove, crushed; salt and pepper

Herby Bean & Feta Salad

■ Cook the pasta in a large saucepan of salted boiling water according to the packet instructions until al dente. Drain, refresh in cold water and drain thoroughly.

■ Meanwhile, cook the broad beans in a separate saucepan of lightly salted boiling water for 4–5 minutes until just tender. Drain and plunge into ice-cold water to cool. Peel off the skins.

■ Make the dressing by whisking together the extra virgin olive oil, sherry vinegar and garlic in a small bowl, then season with salt and pepper.

■ Put the beans in a serving dish and stir in the pasta, tomatoes and herbs. Toss with the dressing and scatter over the feta. Serve immediately.

SERVES 2

Preparation time 10 minutes
Cooking time 55–60 minutes

INGREDIENTS

| 1 | **4 large red peppers** |

| 2 | **1 tablespoon chopped thyme, plus extra to garnish** |

| 3 | **4 plum tomatoes, halved** |

STORECUPBOARD

2 garlic cloves, crushed; 4 tablespoons extra virgin olive oil; 2 tablespoons balsamic vinegar; salt and black pepper

Roasted Stuffed Peppers

■ Cut the red peppers in half lengthways, then scoop out and discard the cores and seeds. Put the pepper halves, cut-sides up, in a roasting tin lined with foil or a ceramic dish. Divide the garlic and thyme between them and season with salt and pepper.

■ Put a tomato half in each pepper and drizzle with the oil and vinegar. Roast in a preheated oven, 220°C (425°F), Gas Mark 7, for 55–60 minutes until the peppers are soft and charred.

Preparation time 10 minutes
Cooking time 20 minutes

INGREDIENTS

1	500 g (1 lb) sweet potatoes, sliced
2	5 spring onions, sliced
3	2 tablespoons chopped fresh coriander
4	4 large eggs, beaten
5	100 g (3½ oz) round goats' cheese with rind, cut into 4 slices

STORE CUPBOARD

1 teaspoon olive oil; black pepper

Sweet Potato & Goats' Cheese Frittata

■ Put the sweet potato slices in a saucepan of boiling water and cook for 7–8 minutes or until just tender, then drain.

■ Heat the oil in a medium nonstick frying pan, add the spring onions and sweet potato slices and fry for 2 minutes.

■ Stir the coriander into the beaten eggs, season with plenty of pepper and pour into the pan. Arrange the slices of goats' cheese on top and continue to cook for 3–4 minutes until almost set.

■ Put the pan under a preheated hot grill and cook for 2–3 minutes until golden and bubbling. Serve immediately.

CHANGE THE FILLING

For butternut squash and feta frittata, replace the sweet potatoes with 500 g (1 lb) cubed butternut squash. Sprinkle 100g (3½ oz) of crumbled feta cheese on top of the frittata in place of the goats' cheese.

Preparation time 25 minutes
Cooking time 1½ hours

INGREDIENTS

1	1 kg (2 lb) beetroot
2	½ teaspoon caraway seeds
3	1 tablespoon chopped lemon thyme, plus extra to garnish
4	40 g (1½ oz) butter, cut into small pieces
5	200 g (7 oz) soft goats' cheese, thinly sliced

STORE CUPBOARD

500 g (1 lb) small onions, quartered; 4 tablespoons olive oil; 75 g (3 oz) plain flour; salt and black pepper

Beetroot & Goats' Cheese Crumble

■ Scrub the beetroot and cut into thin wedges. Place in a shallow ovenproof dish with the onions and drizzle with the oil. Sprinkle with the caraway seeds and season with a little salt and plenty of pepper. Cook in a preheated oven, 200°C (400°F), Gas Mark 6, for about 1 hour until the vegetables are roasted and tender, stirring once or twice during cooking.

■ Meanwhile, place the flour and lemon thyme in a bowl, add the butter and rub in with the fingertips until the mixture resembles fine breadcrumbs.

■ Scatter the goats' cheese over the vegetables and sprinkle with the crumble mixture. Return to the oven for about 25–30 minutes until the topping is pale golden. Sprinkle the crumble with thyme and serve immediately.

Preparation time 10 minutes
Cooking time 10–15 minutes

INGREDIENTS

1 4 courgettes, cut into matchsticks

2 2 celery sticks, cut into matchsticks

3 250 g (8 oz) soft cheese with garlic

4 100 g (3½ oz) walnut pieces

STORE CUPBOARD

3 tablespoons olive oil; 1 onion, chopped; salt
and black pepper

Creamy Courgettes with Walnuts

■ Heat the oil in a large frying pan, add
the onion and cook for 5 minutes until soft.
Add the courgette and celery matchsticks
and cook for 4–5 minutes until soft and
starting to brown.

■ Add the cheese and cook for about
2–3 minutes until melted. Stir in the
walnuts, season to taste with salt and
pepper and serve immediately.

Preparation time 10 minutes
Cooking time 10 minutes

INGREDIENTS

1   15 g (½ oz) butter

2   500 g (1 lb) chestnut mushrooms, sliced

3   2 tablespoons wholegrain mustard

4   250 ml (8 fl oz) crème fraîche

5   3 tablespoons chopped parsley

STORE CUPBOARD

2 tablespoons olive oil; 1 onion, thinly sliced;
4 garlic cloves, finely chopped; salt and
black pepper

Mushroom Stroganoff

■ Heat the butter and olive oil in a large
frying pan, add the onion and garlic and
fry gently until softened and beginning
to brown.

■ Add the mushrooms to the pan and
cook until softened and beginning to
brown. Stir in the mustard and crème
fraîche and just heat through. Season
to taste with salt and pepper, then
serve immediately, garnished with the
chopped parsley.

SERVES 4

Preparation time 10 minutes
Cooking time 10 minutes

INGREDIENTS

1	4 spring onions, thinly sliced
2	200 g (7 oz) can sweetcorn, drained
3	150 g (5 oz) bottled roasted red peppers in oil, drained and cut into strips
4	4 eggs, lightly beaten
5	125 g (4 oz) strong Cheddar cheese, grated

STORE CUPBOARD

2 tablespoons olive oil; salt and black pepper

Sweetcorn & Pepper Frittata

■ Heat the oil in a frying pan with an ovenproof handle, add the spring onions, sweetcorn and red peppers, and cook for 30 seconds.

■ Add the eggs, Cheddar, and salt and pepper to taste and cook over a medium heat for 4–5 minutes or until the base is set.

■ Place the pan under a preheated hot grill and cook the omelette for 3–4 minutes or until golden and set. Cut into wedges and serve immediately.

SERVES 4

Preparation time 15 minutes
Cooking time 10–12 minutes

INGREDIENTS

1	375 g (12 oz) dried rigatoni
2	3 courgettes, cut into 1 cm (½ inch) thick slices
3	2 lemon thyme sprigs
4	200 g (7 oz) feta cheese, cut into cubes
5	12 green olives, pitted and roughly chopped

STORE CUPBOARD

6 tablespoons olive oil; ½ lemon, for squeezing; salt and black pepper

Rigatoni with Courgettes & Feta

■ Cook the pasta in a large saucepan of salted boiling water according to the packet instructions until al dente. Drain thoroughly.

■ Meanwhile, put the courgettes in a large bowl and toss with 1 tablespoon of the oil. Heat a ridged griddle pan over a high heat until smoking. Add the courgette slices and cook for 2–3 minutes on each side until lightly charred and tender.

■ Return the courgette slices to the bowl. Drizzle with the remaining oil, scatter over the lemon thyme sprigs and squeeze over the juice from the lemon half. Season with salt and pepper.

■ Drain the pasta thoroughly and add it to the bowl with the feta and olives. Toss well to combine and serve the pasta immediately.

USE ARTICHOKES & TALEGGIO

For rigatoni with artichoke hearts
and taleggio, use 2 × 400 g (13 oz)
cans artichoke hearts instead of
the courgettes. Drain and halve
the artichoke hearts, toss with
1 tablespoon oil and stir-fry with
1 tablespoon finely chopped
rosemary for 2 minutes. Omit
the lemon juice. Combine with
the green olives and 150 g (5 oz)
taleggio, cut into cubes, and the
cooked pasta.

SERVES 4

Preparation time 10 minutes, plus standing
Cooking time 10–12 minutes

INGREDIENTS

1	750 g (1½ lb) very ripe tomatoes, quartered
2	10 basil leaves
3	2 teaspoons fennel seeds
4	400 g (13 oz) dried spaghetti
5	2 × 150 g (5 oz) buffalo mozzarella cheese balls, cut into cubes

STORE CUPBOARD

2 garlic cloves, peeled; 5 tablespoons extra virgin olive oil; salt and black pepper

No-cook-tomato Spaghetti

■ Put the tomatoes, garlic cloves and basil in a food processor and process until the tomatoes are finely chopped but not smooth. Transfer to a large bowl and add the fennel seeds and oil.

■ Season with salt and pepper. Leave the flavours to infuse for at least 15 minutes before cooking the pasta.

■ Cook the pasta in a large saucepan of salted boiling water according to the packet instructions until al dente. Drain, stir into the prepared tomato sauce, then toss in the mozzarella. Serve immediately.

TRY A DIFFERENT PASTA

For herby no-cook tomato orecchiette, replace 125 g (4 oz) of the tomatoes with sun-blush tomatoes. Coarsely shred 150 g (5 oz) rocket and mix with the leaves from 4 sprigs of thyme. Toss with cooked orechiette and serve with mozzarella, as in the main recipe.

SERVES 6

Preparation time 40 minutes
Cooking time 50 minutes, plus standing

INGREDIENTS

1 400 g (13 oz) can chopped tomatoes

2 6 aubergines

3 250 g (8 oz) grated Cheddar cheese

4 50 g (2 oz) grated Parmesan cheese

STORE CUPBOARD

4 tablespoons olive oil; 1 large onion, chopped; 2 garlic cloves, finely chopped; salt and black pepper

Melanzane Parmigiana

■ To make the tomato sauce, heat half the olive oil in a frying pan. Fry the onion for about 5 minutes, then add the garlic and tomatoes and cook gently for 10 minutes. Season well with salt and pepper and keep warm.

■ Trim the ends off the aubergines and cut them lengthways into thick slices. Sprinkle generously with salt and set side for about 10 minutes. Wash well, drain and pat dry on kitchen paper.

■ Brush the aubergine slices with the remaining oil and place them on 2 large baking sheets. Roast the aubergines in a preheated oven, 200°C (400°F), Gas Mark 6, for 10 minutes on each side until golden and tender. Do not turn off the oven.

■ Spoon a little of the tomato sauce into an ovenproof dish, then top with a layer of roasted aubergine and some of the Cheddar. Continue with the layers, finishing with the Cheddar. Sprinkle over the Parmesan and bake for 30 minutes until bubbling and golden. Remove from the oven and leave to stand for 5–10 minutes.

SERVES 4

Preparation time 15 minutes
Cooking time 15 minutes

INGREDIENTS

| 1 | 750 g (1½ lb) Desiree potatoes, peeled |

| 2 | 2 teaspoons chopped rosemary |

| 3 | 4 large eggs |

| 4 | chopped parsley, to garnish |

STORE CUPBOARD

1 onion, thinly sliced; 4 tablespoons olive oil;
salt and black pepper

Potato Rösti with Frazzled Eggs

■ Using a box grater, coarsely grate the potatoes. Wrap in a clean tea towel and squeeze out the excess liquid over the sink. Transfer to a bowl and stir in the onion, rosemary and salt and pepper.

■ Heat half the oil in a large frying pan. Divide the potato mixture into quarters and spoon into 4 × 12 cm (5 inch) mounds in the pan, pressing down to form patties. Cook over a medium heat for 5 minutes on each side, transfer to warmed serving plates and keep warm in a moderate oven.

■ Heat the remaining oil in the frying pan for about 1 minute until very hot, add the eggs, 2 at a time, and fry until the whites are bubbly and crisp looking. Serve the eggs on the rösti, garnished with chopped parsley.

TRY POACHING THE EGGS

For rösti with poached eggs, bring a saucepan of lightly salted water to a simmer and add 1 tablespoon white vinegar. Crack an egg into a cup. Swirl the simmering water with a large spoon, gently drop the egg into the centre and cook for 2–3 minutes. Carefully remove with a slotted spoon. Repeat with the remaining eggs and finish as in the main recipe.

SERVES 4

Preparation time 5 minutes
Cooking time 30 minutes

INGREDIENTS

1	2 × 400 g (13 oz) cans chopped tomatoes
2	¼ teaspoon dried chilli flakes
3	2 tablespoons chopped fresh basil
4	400 g (13 oz) dried spaghetti
5	25 g (1 oz) freshly grated Parmesan cheese, to serve

STORE CUPBOARD

2 tablespoons extra virgin olive oil; 2 large garlic cloves, crushed; 1 teaspoon caster sugar; salt and black pepper

Spaghetti with Easy Tomato Sauce

■ To make the sauce, place the tomatoes, oil, garlic, sugar and chilli flakes in a saucepan. Season with salt and pepper and bring to the boil. Lower the heat and simmer gently for 20–30 minutes until thickened and full of flavour.

■ Stir in the basil and adjust the seasoning. Keep warm.

■ Meanwhile, cook the pasta into a saucepan of lightly salted, boiling water for 10–12 minutes, or according to the packet instructions, until al dente. Drain the pasta and divide between bowls, spoon over the sauce and serve with Parmesan cheese.

AN ALTERNATIVE SAUCE

For tomato, chilli and olive sauce,
follow the main recipe but add
½ teaspoon dried chilli flakes. Stir
in 125 g (4 oz) pitted black olives
just before the end of cooking and
heat through.

Preparation time 10 minutes
Cooking time 25 minutes

INGREDIENTS

1	**3 peppers of mixed colours, cored, deseeded and sliced into rings**
2	**4 tomatoes, chopped**
3	**200 g (7 oz) feta cheese, cubed**
4	**1 teaspoon dried oregano**
5	**chopped flat leaf parsley, to garnish**

STORE CUPBOARD

4 tablespoons olive oil; 1 onion, thinly sliced;
4 garlic cloves, crushed; salt and black pepper

Greek Vegetable Casserole

■ Heat 3 tablespoons of the oil in a flameproof casserole, add the onion, peppers and garlic and cook until soft and starting to brown. Add the tomatoes and cook for a few minutes until softened. Mix in the feta and oregano, season to taste with salt and pepper and drizzle with the remaining oil.

■ Cover and cook in a preheated oven, 200°C (400°F), Gas Mark 6, for 15 minutes. Garnish with the parsley and serve.

SERVES 4

Preparation time 10 minutes
Cooking time 10–15 minutes

INGREDIENTS

1	6 large ripe plum tomatoes
2	1 red chilli, deseeded and finely diced
3	25 g (1 oz) fresh basil leaves, finely chopped
4	375 g (12 oz) dried rigatoni
5	grated Parmesan cheese, to serve (optional)

STORE CUPBOARD

1 tablespoon extra-virgin olive oil; 2 garlic cloves, finely diced; 75 ml (3 fl oz) vegetable stock; salt and pepper

Rigatoni with Fresh Tomato, Chilli & Basil

■ Place the tomatoes in a bowl and pour over boiling water to cover. Leave for about 1–2 minutes, then drain, cut across the stem end of each tomato, and peel off the skins.

■ When cool enough to handle, cut the tomatoes in half horizontally and shake or gently spoon out the seeds then finely dice the flesh.

■ Heat the oil in a large, nonstick frying pan and add the garlic and chilli. Cook on a medium-low heat for 1–2 minutes or until the garlic is fragrant but not browned.

■ Add the tomatoes, vegetable stock and basil, season well and cook gently for about 6–8 minutes or until thickened, stirring often.

■ Meanwhile, cook the rigatoni in a large saucepan of lightly salted boiling water according to the packet instructions, until al dente. Drain and toss into the tomato sauce mixture.

■ Spoon into warmed bowls and serve with grated Parmesan, if desired.

HEALTHY OPTIONS

Preparation time 5 minutes
Cooking time 5 minutes

INGREDIENTS

| 1 | ½ red chilli, sliced into rings |

| 2 | 1 tablespoon chopped fresh root ginger |

| 3 | 500 g (1 lb) pak choi, leaves separated |

STORE CUPBOARD

1 tablespoon groundnut oil; salt; ¼ teaspoon
sesame oil

Pak Choi with Chilli & Ginger

■ Heat the groundnut oil in a wok over
a high heat until the oil starts to shimmer.
Add the chilli, ginger and a pinch of salt
and stir-fry for 15 seconds.

■ Tip the pak choi into the wok and
stir-fry for 1 minute, then add 100ml
(3½ fl oz) water and continue stirring
until the pak choi is tender and the water
has evaporated. Toss in the sesame oil
and serve immediately.

Preparation time 10 minutes, plus cooling
Cooking time 10 minutes

INGREDIENTS

| **1** | **4 shallots, finely chopped** |

| **2** | **1 teaspoon chopped rosemary, plus extra sprigs to garnish** |

| **3** | **2 × 400 g (13 oz) cans butter beans** |

| **4** | **toasted ciabatta, to serve** |

STORE CUPBOARD

6 tablespoons extra virgin olive oil, plus extra to serve; 2 large garlic cloves, crushed; grated rind and juice of ½ lemon; salt and black pepper

Bean, Lemon & Rosemary Hummus

■ Heat the oil in a frying pan, add the shallots, garlic, chopped rosemary and lemon rind and cook over a low heat, stirring occasionally, for 10 minutes until the shallots are softened. Leave to cool.

■ Transfer the shallot mixture to a blender or food processor, add the butter beans and lemon juice, and process until smooth.

■ Spread the hummus on to toasted ciabatta, garnish with rosemary sprigs and serve drizzled with oil.

USE CHICKPEAS & CHILLI

For chickpea and chilli hummus, put 2 × 400 g (13 oz) cans drained chickpeas in a food processor with 2 deseeded and chopped red chillies, 1 large crushed garlic clove, 2 tablespoons lemon juice and salt and pepper to taste. Process with enough extra virgin olive oil to form a soft paste. Serve as a dip with vegetable crudités.

Preparation time 10 minutes
Cooking time 2 hours

INGREDIENTS

1	2 × 400 g (13 oz) cans borlotti beans, drained
2	300 ml (½ pint) passata (sieved tomatoes)
3	2 tablespoons molasses or black treacle
4	2 tablespoons tomato purée
5	1 tablespoon Dijon mustard

STORE CUPBOARD

1 garlic clove, crushed; 1 onion, finely chopped; 450 ml (¾ pint) vegetable stock; 2 tablespoons soft dark brown sugar; 1 tablespoon red wine vinegar; salt and black pepper

Home Baked Beans

■ Put all the ingredients in a flameproof casserole and season with salt and pepper. Cover and bring slowly to the boil.

■ Bake in a preheated oven, 160°C (325°F), Gas Mark 3, for 1½ hours. Remove the lid and bake for a further 30 minutes until the sauce is syrupy. Serve with hot buttered toast, if liked, or jacket potatoes (see opposite).

JUST ADD JACKETS

Scrub 4 Desiree or King Edward
potatoes, about 250 g (8 oz) each,
then bake in a preheated oven, 200°C
(400°F), Gas Mark 6, for about 1 hour
until cooked through. Cut lengthways
in half, season with salt and pepper
and spoon over the beans. Grate
over a little Cheddar before serving.
The home baked beans are even
better made a day ahead and heated
through before serving.

Preparation time 10 minutes, plus soaking

INGREDIENTS

1	150 g (5 oz) bulgar wheat
2	75 g (3 oz) unsalted, shelled pistachio nuts
3	25 g (1 oz) flat leaf parsley, chopped
4	15 g (½ oz) mint, chopped
5	150 g (5 oz) ready-to-eat prunes, sliced

STORE CUPBOARD

1 small red onion, finely chopped; 3 garlic cloves, crushed; finely grated rind and juice of 1 lemon or lime; 4 tablespoons olive oil; salt and black pepper

Tabbouleh with Fruit & Nuts

■ Put the bulgar wheat into a bowl, cover with plenty of boiling water and leave to soak for 15 minutes.

■ Meanwhile, put the pistachio nuts in a separate bowl and cover with boiling water. Leave to stand for 1 minute, then drain. Rub the nuts between several thicknesses of kitchen paper to remove most of the skins, then peel away any remaining skins with your fingers.

■ Mix the nuts with the onion, garlic, parsley, mint, lemon or lime rind and juice and prunes in a large bowl.

■ Drain the bulgar wheat thoroughly in a sieve, pressing out as much moisture as possible with the back of a spoon. Add to the other ingredients with the oil and toss together. Season to taste with salt and pepper and chill until ready to serve.

A TRADITIONAL TABBOULEH

For classic tabbouleh, omit the nuts and prunes and add 6 chopped tomatoes and 50 g (2 oz) chopped black olives. Use only 2 garlic cloves and be sure to use a lemon not a lime.

Preparation time 10 minutes
Cooking time 15–20 minutes

INGREDIENTS

1   50 g (2 oz) sunflower or pumpkin seeds

2   500 g (1 lb) wholewheat spaghetti

3   1 small bunch of basil

4   75 g (3 oz) rocket leaves

5   25 g (1 oz) Parmesan-style cheese, finely grated, plus extra to serve (optional)

STORE CUPBOARD

1 small garlic clove, roughly chopped;
6 tablespoons olive oil; 1 tablespoon lemon
juice; salt and black pepper

Basil & Rocket Pesto with Spaghetti

■ Place the seeds in a small, dry frying pan and toast gently for 3–4 minutes, shaking the pan frequently, until lightly toasted and golden. Tip onto a plate to cool.

■ Cook the spaghetti in a large saucepan of lightly salted boiling water for 11–12 minutes, or according to packet instructions, until al dente.

■ Meanwhile, crush the garlic together with a generous pinch of sea salt using a pestle and mortar. Add the basil and rocket leaves, and pound until crushed to a coarse paste.

■ Add the toasted seeds and pound to a paste, then transfer to a bowl and stir in the cheese, olive oil and lemon juice. Season to taste with plenty of black pepper and more salt, if necessary.

■ Drain the pasta and toss immediately with the pesto.

■ Divide between 4 shallow bowls and serve with extra cheese, if desired.

Preparation time 10 minutes, plus standing
Cooking time 10 minutes

INGREDIENTS

1 600 g (1 lb 3½ oz) button mushrooms, halved

2 8 plum tomatoes, roughly chopped or 400 g (13 oz) can chopped tomatoes

3 100 g (3½ oz) pitted black olives

4 chopped parsley, to garnish

STORE CUPBOARD

8 tablespoons olive oil; 2 large onions, sliced; 3 garlic cloves, finely chopped; 2 tablespoons white wine vinegar; salt and black pepper

Mushrooms à la Grecque

■ Heat 2 tablespoons of the oil in a large frying pan, add the onions and garlic and cook until soft and starting to brown. Add the mushrooms and tomatoes and cook, stirring gently, for 4–5 minutes. Remove from the heat.

■ Transfer the mushroom mixture to a serving dish and garnish with the olives.

■ Whisk the remaining oil with the vinegar in a small bowl, season to taste with salt and pepper and drizzle over the salad. Garnish with the chopped parsley, cover and leave to stand at room temperature for 30 minutes to allow the flavours to mingle before serving.

SERVES 4

Preparation time 5 minutes
Cooking time 10 minutes

INGREDIENTS

1	375 g (12 oz) quick-cook pasta
2	400 g (13 oz) cooked beetroot
3	200 ml (7 fl oz) crème fraîche
4	4 tablespoons chopped chives
5	4 tablespoons chopped dill

STORE CUPBOARD

salt and black pepper

Beetroot Pasta with Herbs

- Cook the pasta in a large saucepan of lightly salted boiling water according to the packet instructions, until al dente.

- Meanwhile, finely dice the beetroot and add to the pasta for the last minute of the cooking time.

- Drain the pasta and beetroot and return to the saucepan. Stir in the crème fraîche and herbs.

- Season and serve immediately.

Preparation time 10 minutes
Cooking time 35 minutes

INGREDIENTS

1   **2 tablespoons mild curry paste**

2   **400 g (13 oz) can chopped tomatoes**

3   **400 g (13 oz) can chickpeas, drained**

4   **100 g (3½ oz) curly kale**

STORE CUPBOARD

3 tablespoons vegetable oil; 3 red onions, cut into wedges; 300 ml (½ pint) vegetable stock; 2 teaspoons soft light brown sugar; salt and black pepper

Spiced Chickpeas with Kale

■ Heat the oil in a large saucepan and fry the onions for 5 minutes until beginning to colour. Stir in the curry paste and then the tomatoes, chickpeas, stock and sugar.

■ Bring to the boil, then reduce the heat, cover and simmer gently for 20 minutes.

■ Stir in the kale and cook gently for a further 10 minutes. Season to taste with salt and pepper and serve.

SERVES 4–6

Preparation time 10 minutes, plus cooling
Cooking time 45 minutes

INGREDIENTS

1   **250 g (8 oz) waxy potatoes such as Charlotte, peeled and cut into 1.5 cm (¾ inch) dice**

2   **200 g (7 oz) baby spinach leaves**

3   **6 large eggs**

STORE CUPBOARD

2 tablespoons olive oil; 1 small onion, finely chopped; salt and black pepper

Spinach & Potato Omelette

■ Cook the potatoes in a saucepan of lightly salted boiling water until just tender; be careful not to overcook. Drain, then leave to cool.

■ Rinse the spinach and drain off the excess water in a colander. Put in a dry frying pan over a medium heat with just the water clinging to the leaves from rinsing, cover and cook for 2–3 minutes, shaking the pan from time to time, until just wilted. Squeeze out any remaining water, then roughly chop. Set aside.

■ Heat the oil in a 20 cm (8 inch) nonstick frying pan with a flameproof handle (or cover the handle with foil) over a low heat. Add the onion and cook, stirring occasionally, for 8–10 minutes until softened. Add the cooled potatoes and cook, stirring, for 2–3 minutes. Add the reserved spinach and stir.

■ Beat the eggs lightly in a bowl and season with salt and pepper. Pour into the pan over the vegetables and cook over a low heat, shaking frequently, for about 10–12 minutes until set on the bottom.

■ Put the pan under a preheated medium grill and cook for 2–3 minutes or until the top is set and lightly browned. Remove from the heat and leave to rest for about 3–4 minutes before turning out on to a chopping board. Cut into wedges and serve immediately.

Preparation time 15 minutes
Cooking time 20–25 minutes

INGREDIENTS

1	1 kg (2 lb) pumpkin

2	50 g (2 oz) walnuts, toasted

3	2 spring onions, trimmed and chopped

4	50 g (2 oz) rocket leaves, plus extra to serve

STORECUPBOARD

1 large garlic clove, crushed; 3 tablespoons extra virgin olive oil, plus extra for brushing; 3 tablespoons walnut oil; salt and black pepper

Pumpkin with Walnut Pesto

■ Cut the pumpkin into 8 wedges. Remove the seeds and fibre but leave the skin on. Brush all over with olive oil, season with salt and pepper and spread out on a large baking sheet. Roast in a preheated oven, 220°C (425°F), Gas Mark 7, for about 20–25 minutes until tender, turning halfway through.

■ Meanwhile, make the pesto. Put the walnuts, spring onions, garlic and rocket in a food processor and process until finely chopped. With the motor running, gradually drizzle in the oils. Season the pesto with salt and pepper.

■ Serve the roasted pumpkin with the pesto and extra rocket leaves.

Preparation time 5 minutes
Cooking time about 12 minutes

INGREDIENTS

1	**200 g (7 oz) dried papperdelle or other ribbon pasta**
2	**50 g (2 oz) butter**
3	**2 tablespoons chopped dill**
4	**50 g (2 oz) Parmesan cheese, freshly grated**
5	**50 g (2 oz) pea shoots, thick stalks discarded**

STORE CUPBOARD

1 garlic clove, crushed; lemon wedges, for squeezing over; salt and black pepper

Pappardelle with Pea Shoots & Dill

■ Cook the pasta in a large saucepan of lightly salted boiling water for about 8–10 minutes, or according to the packet instructions, until al dente. Drain and return to the pan.

■ Dot the butter on to the hot pasta and add the garlic, dill, Parmesan and a little salt and pepper. Stir until well mixed, then add the pea shoots and stir until slightly wilted and distributed through the pasta.

■ Serve immediately with lemon wedges for squeezing over the pasta.

Preparation time 5 minutes
Cooking time 20 minutes

INGREDIENTS

1	2 leeks, cut into 1 cm (½ inch) pieces
2	1 orange pepper, deseeded and cut into 1 cm (½ inch) chunks
3	1 red pepper, deseeded and cut into 1 cm (½ inch) chunks
4	handful of flat leaf parsley, chopped

STORE CUPBOARD

2 tablespoons olive oil; 3 tablespoons balsamic vinegar; salt and black pepper

Balsamic Braised Leeks & Peppers

■ Heat the oil in a saucepan, add the leeks and orange and red peppers and stir well.

■ Cover the pan and cook very gently for 10 minutes. Add the balsamic vinegar and cook for a further 10 minutes without a lid. The vegetables should be brown from the vinegar and all the liquid should have evaporated.

■ Season well, then stir in the chopped parsley just before serving.

Preparation time 5 minutes
Cooking time 45–50 minutes

INGREDIENTS

1	4 sweet potatoes, about 250 g (8 oz) each, scrubbed
2	200 g (7 oz) soured cream
3	2 spring onions, trimmed and finely chopped
4	1 tablespoon chopped chives
5	50 g (2 oz) butter

STORE CUPBOARD

salt and black pepper

Baked Sweet Potatoes

■ Put the potatoes in a roasting tin and roast in a preheated oven, 220°C (425°F), Gas Mark 7, for 45–50 minutes until cooked through.

■ Meanwhile, combine the soured cream, spring onions and salt and pepper in a small bowl.

■ Cut the baked potatoes in half lengthways, top with the butter and spoon over the soured cream mixture. Sprinkle with the chopped chives and serve immediately.

SWEET POTATO SKINS

For crispy sweet potato skins, allow the baked sweet potatoes to cool, cut into wedges and cut out some of the soft potato, leaving a good lining inside the skin. Deep-fry in hot oil for 4–5 minutes until crisp. Serve with soured cream and chopped chives to dip.

Preparation time 10 minutes
Cooking time 15–18 minutes

INGREDIENTS

1 450 g (14½ oz) dried spaghetti

2 350 g (11½ oz) fresh or frozen shelled broad beans

3 pinch of dried chilli flakes

4 2 tablespoons basil leaves

5 freshly grated Parmesan or pecorino cheese, to serve (optional)

STORECUPBOARD

4 tablespoons extra virgin olive oil; 3 garlic cloves, finely chopped; grated rind and juice of 1 lemon; salt and black pepper

Broad Bean & Lemon Spaghetti

■ Cook the pasta in a large saucepan of lightly salted boiling water for about 10–12 minutes, or according to the packet instructions, until al dente. Drain, reserving 4 tablespoons of the cooking water, and return the pasta to the pan.

■ Cook the broad beans in a separate saucepan of salted boiling water for 3–4 minutes. Drain well.

■ Meanwhile, heat the oil in a frying pan, add the garlic, chilli flakes, lemon rind and salt and pepper and cook over a low heat, stirring, for 3–4 minutes until the garlic is soft but not browned.

■ Scrape the oil mixture into the pasta with the beans, reserved pasta cooking water, lemon juice and basil and stir over a medium heat until heated through. Serve with grated Parmesan or pecorino.

TRY IT WITH PEAS & MINT

For spaghetti with peas and mint, replace the broad beans with 350 g (11½ oz) of shelled fresh peas and cook as in the recipe above, adding 2 tablespoons chopped mint instead of the basil just before serving. Frozen petit pois can be used instead of fresh peas.

SERVES 4

Preparation time 10 minutes
Cooking time 30 minutes

INGREDIENTS

1	100 g (3½ oz) Puy lentils
2	1 tablespoon tomato purée
3	100 g (3½ oz) bulgar wheat
4	1 bunch of mint, chopped
5	3 tomatoes, finely chopped

STORE CUPBOARD

750 ml (1¼ pints) vegetable stock; juice of 1 lemon; 1 tablespoon olive oil; 2 onions, sliced; 1 teaspoon granulated sugar; salt and black pepper

Lebanese Lentil & Bulgar Salad

■ Put the lentils, tomato purée and stock in a saucepan and bring to the boil. Reduce the heat, cover tightly and simmer for 20 minutes. Add the bulgar wheat and lemon juice and season to taste with salt and pepper. Cook for 10 minutes until all the stock has been absorbed.

■ Meanwhile, heat the oil in a frying pan, add the onions and sugar and cook over a low heat until deep brown and caramelized.

■ Stir the mint into the lentil and bulgar wheat mixture, then serve warm, topped with the fried onions and chopped tomato.

FOOD FOR FRIENDS

SERVES 4

Preparation time 15 minutes, plus cooling
Cooking time 40 minutes

INGREDIENTS

1	25 g (1 oz) unsalted butter
2	2 tablespoons chopped thyme, plus a few extra leaves to garnish
3	320 g (10½ oz) sheet of ready-rolled puff pastry, defrosted if frozen
4	2 × 100 g (3½ oz) round goats' cheeses, each sliced into 4

STORE CUPBOARD

4 large red onions, thinly sliced; 1 teaspoon soft light brown sugar; 2 teaspoons balsamic vinegar

Red Onion & Goats' Cheese Tart

■ Melt the butter in a large frying pan, add the onions, sugar and chopped thyme and cook gently for 20 minutes, stirring occasionally, until the onions start to caramelize. Stir in the vinegar and cook for 1 minute. Leave to cool slightly.

■ Unroll the pastry sheet and place on a nonstick baking sheet. Using a sharp knife, score a line along each side of the sheet 2.5 cm (1 inch) from the edge, being careful not to cut all the way through the pastry.

■ Spoon the caramelized onions over the pastry, within the scored border, then top with the goats' cheese slices.

■ Bake in a preheated oven, 200°C (400°F), Gas Mark 6, for 20 minutes until the pastry is risen and golden. Serve garnished with a few thyme leaves.

Preparation time 15 minutes
Cooking time 40–45 minutes, plus re-heat
  20 minutes

INGREDIENTS

1	500 g (1 lb) plum tomatoes
2	1 red pepper, cored, deseeded and quartered
3	small bunch of sage
4	200 g (7 oz) easy-cook long-grain white and wild rice mixed

STORE CUPBOARD

1 onion, roughly chopped; 2 tablespoons olive oil;
salt and black pepper

Sage & Tomato Pilaf

■ Cut each tomato into 8 and thickly slice the pepper quarters. Place in a roasting tin with the onion, then drizzle with the oil and season well. Tear some of the sage into pieces and sprinkle over the vegetables. Roast in a preheated oven, 200°C (400°F), Gas Mark 6, for 40–45 minutes until soft.

■ Meanwhile, cook the rice in a saucepan of boiling water for 15 minutes until only just cooked. Drain, rinse in cold water and drain again. Mix the rice into the cooked tomatoes and peppers, then cover with foil. Allow to cool and chill until required.

■ When ready to serve, reheat in a preheated oven, 180°C (350°F), Gas Mark 4, still covered with foil for 20 minutes until piping hot. Stir well, then spoon into bowls and sprinkle with the remaining sage leaves. Serve immediately.

TRY A NEW FLAVOUR

For pumpkin and blue cheese pilaf,
Roast 500 g (1 lb) peeled, deseeded
and diced pumpkin (or butternut
squash) with 3 halved plum
tomatoes and onion as in the main
recipe. Cook the rice for 15 minutes,
then drain, allow to cool and chill
until required. Reheat as in the main
recipe, then top with 125 g (4 oz)
crumbled St Agur or other blue
cheese and serve.

SERVES 4

Preparation time 20 minutes
Cooking time 25–30 minutes

INGREDIENTS

1   250 g (8 oz) pack of 6 fresh lasagne sheets

2   500 g (1 lb) mixed mushrooms such as shiitake, oyster and chestnut, sliced

3   200 g (7 oz) mascarpone cheese

4   125 g (4 oz) baby spinach leaves

5   150 g (5 oz) taleggio cheese, derinded and cut into cubes

STORE CUPBOARD

3 tablespoons olive oil; 2 garlic cloves, finely chopped; salt and black pepper

Mushroom & Spinach Lasagne

■ Place the lasagne sheets in a large roasting tray and cover with boiling water. Leave to stand for 5 minutes, or until tender, then drain off the water.

■ Heat the oil in a large frying pan and fry the mushrooms for 5 minutes. Add the garlic and mascarpone and turn up the heat. Cook for another 1 minute until the sauce is thick. Season with salt and pepper. Steam the spinach for 2 minutes or microwave until just wilted.

■ Oil an ovenproof dish about the size of 2 of the lasagne sheets and place 2 of the lasagne sheets over the base, slightly overlapping. Reserve one-third of the taleggio for the top, sprinkle a little over the pasta base with one third of the mushroom sauce and one-third of the spinach leaves. Repeat with 2 more layers, topping the final layer of lasagne sheets with the remaining mushroom sauce, spinach and taleggio.

■ Bake in a preheated oven, 200°C (400°F), Gas Mark 6, for 15–20 minutes until the cheese is golden and the lasagne piping hot.

SERVES 4

Preparation time 15 minutes
Cooking time 10 minutes

INGREDIENTS

1   12 slices of thin baguette

2   200 g (7 oz) marinated, pitted black olives

3   small bunch of basil

4   25 g (1 oz) pecorino or Parmesan cheese, grated

STORE CUPBOARD

1 garlic clove, halved; 2 tablespoons olive oil

Black Olive Tapenade Toasts

■ Toast the bread lightly on both sides then rub one side with the garlic. Transfer to a baking sheet.

■ Finely chop the olives in a blender or food processor, then add the oil and most of the basil and blend again to make a coarse paste. Spread over the garlic toasts. Cover loosely and chill until required.

■ When ready to serve, remove the cover and cook the toasts in a preheated oven, 190°C (375°F), Gas Mark 5, for 10 minutes. Arrange on a serving plate and sprinkle with the pecorino or Parmesan and the remaining basil leaves.

SERVES 4

Preparation time 25 minutes
Cooking time 12 minutes, plus finishing

INGREDIENTS

1 500 g (1 lb) shallots, peeled

2 50 g (2 oz) butter

3 a few thyme sprigs

4 250 g (8 oz) puff pastry, thawed if frozen

STORE CUPBOARD

2 tablespoons light muscovado sugar;
3 tablespoons cider vinegar; flour, for dusting;
salt and black pepper

Shallot Tart Tatin

■ Cut any large shallots in half. Melt the butter in a 20 cm (8 inch) frying pan. Add the shallots and fry over a medium heat for 5 minutes until just beginning to colour.

■ Add the sugar and fry for 5 more minutes or until caramelized, turning from time to time so that the shallots cook evenly. Add the vinegar, leaves from the thyme sprigs and some seasoning and cook for 2 minutes.

■ If your frying pan has a metal handle, leave the shallots to cool for 20 minutes in the pan, if not transfer to a heavy based 20 cm (8 inch) buttered round cake tin.

■ Roll out the pastry on a lightly floured surface and trim to a 20 cm (8 inch) circle. Arrange on top of the onions and tuck down the sides of the frying pan or cake tin. Cover and chill until required.

■ When ready to serve, remove the cover and bake in a preheated oven, 200°C (400°F), Gas Mark 6, for 25–30 minutes until the pastry is well risen and golden. Leave to stand for 5 minutes, then loosen the edges with a knife. Cover with a serving plate or chopping board and invert the pan or cake tin on to the plate, then remove. Serve warm, cut into wedges with rocket leaves, if liked.

SERVES 4

Preparation time 15 minutes
Cooking time 12 minutes

INGREDIENTS

1   45 g (1½ oz) chopped flat leaf parsley

2   6 large courgettes, thickly sliced

3   8 spring onions, finely sliced

4   400 g (13 oz) dried linguine

5   fresh Parmesan cheese shavings, to serve

STORE CUPBOARD

3 tablespoons olive oil; finely grated rind of
2 unwaxed lemons; 2 garlic cloves, crushed

Courgette & Gremolata Linguine

■ To make the gremolata, mix 1 tablespoon of olive oil, the lemon rind, parsley and garlic together in a bowl.

■ Heat the remaining oil in a nonstick frying pan over a high heat, add the courgettes and cook, stirring frequently, for 10 minutes, or until browned. Add the spring onions and cook, stirring, for about 1–2 minutes.

■ Meanwhile, cook the pasta in a large saucepan of lightly salted boiling water according to the packet instructions, until al dente.

■ Drain the pasta thoroughly and tip into a serving bowl. Add the courgette mixture and the gremolata and toss well. Serve immediately with a scattering of Parmesan shavings.

ASIAN FLAVOURS

For green bean linguine with an oriental gremolata, use finely grated lime rind in place of the lemon rind and fresh coriander instead of the parsley in the gremolata. Omit the courgettes and replace them with 300 g (10 oz) fine green beans, cut into 2.5 cm (1 inch) lengths. Boil for 3–5 minutes. Fry the drained beans and the spring onions for 1 minute.

Preparation time 5–10 minutes

INGREDIENTS

1	625 g (1¼ lb) cooked soba noodles
2	2 carrots, finely julienned
3	6 spring onions, finely shredded
4	1 red pepper, finely sliced
5	4 tablespoons dark soy sauce

STORE CUPBOARD

3 tablespoons sesame oil; 3 tablespoons sesame oil; 1 tablespoon caster sugar; 1 teaspoon chilli oil

Cold Asian Summer Soba Noodle Salad

■ Place the soba noodles in a wide bowl with the carrots, spring onions and pepper.

■ In a separate bowl, mix together the soy sauce, sesame oil, sugar and chilli oil, then pour over the noodle mixture.

■ Toss to mix well and serve chilled or at room temperature.

SERVES 4

Preparation time 10 minutes
Cooking time 15 minutes

INGREDIENTS

1	250 g (8 oz) mixed long grain and wild rice
2	100 g (3½ oz) fine green beans
3	125 g (4 oz) goats' cheese, sliced
4	8 baby plum tomatoes, halved
5	small bunch of basil

STORE CUPBOARD

4 tablespoons olive oil; 3 red onions, thinly sliced; 150 ml (5 fl oz) balsamic vinegar; salt and black pepper

Wild Rice & Goats' Cheese Salad

■ Cook the rice in lightly salted boiling water for about 15 minutes until tender or according to the instructions on the packet. Add the green beans for the final 2 minutes of cooking. Drain and set aside.

■ Meanwhile, heat the oil in a large frying pan and cook the onions gently for about 12 minutes or until soft and golden. Add the balsamic vinegar, season with salt and pepper and allow to bubble gently for about 2–3 minutes until the mixture thickens slightly.

■ Stir the onions into the rice and beans and leave to cool. Once cool, scatter over the cheese and tomatoes and basil leaves and serve.

TRY A PEARL BARLEY SALAD

For pearl barley salad with smoked cheese, replace the rice with 250 g (8 oz) of pearl barley and cook in boiling water for 25–35 minutes until tender, then drain. Substitute the goats' cheese for 125 g (4 oz) diced smoked cheese.

Preparation time 10 minutes
Cooking time 10–12 minutes

INGREDIENTS

1	**400–600 g (13–1 lb 2 oz) dried pasta twists, such as fusilli**
2	**3 ripe tomatoes**
3	**50 g (2 oz) rocket leaves**
4	**100 g (3½ oz) pine nuts**
5	**basil leaves, to garnish**

STORE CUPBOARD

4 garlic cloves, peeled; 150 ml (¼ pint) olive oil; salt and black pepper

Tomato, Pine Nut & Rocket Pesto

■ Cook the pasta in a large saucepan of salted boiling water according to the packet instructions until al dente.

■ Meanwhile, finely chop the tomatoes, garlic cloves, rocket and pine nuts by hand, then stir in the oil. Season with salt and pepper. Transfer to a bowl.

■ Drain the pasta, add to the bowl with the pesto and toss to combine. Serve immediately, garnished with a few basil leaves.

MAKE AN ALMOND PESTO

For tomato, parsley and almond pesto, put 4 ripe tomatoes, 2 cloves garlic, 50 g (2 oz) parsley, 100 g (3½ oz) almonds and 150 ml (½ pint) olive oil in a food processor and process until smooth.

SERVES 4

Preparation time 15 minutes
Cooking time 10 minutes

INGREDIENTS

1 500 g (1 lb) couscous

2 1 pomegranate

3 50 g (2 oz) pine nuts, toasted

4 3 tablespoons chopped flat leaf parsley

5 3 tablespoons chopped fresh coriander

STORE CUPBOARD

2 tablespoons olive oil; 1 mild onion, chopped;
2 garlic cloves, crushed; 300 ml (½ pint)
vegetable stock; grated rind and juice of
1 lemon; salt and black pepper

Pilaf with Nuts, Lemon & Herbs

■ Heat the oil in a large frying pan and cook the onion and garlic for 5 minutes or until soft. Add the stock and heat, then add the couscous. Stir, cover and leave to steam over gentle heat for 5 minutes.

■ Meanwhile, take the seeds from the pomegranate, working over a bowl to catch any juice.

■ When the couscous is ready, stir in the pine nuts and herbs and a little salt and pepper.

■ Mix together the pomegranate seeds and juice and lemon rind and juice. Spoon over the couscous just before serving with the halloumi (see opposite), if you like.

QUICK & EASY HALLOUMI

For grilled marinated halloumi, slice
250 g (8 oz) halloumi into 8 pieces
and marinate in the juice of 1 lemon,
a dash of olive oil and 1 fresh green
chilli, finely chopped. Leave for
20 minutes before grilling until
brown and crisp. Serve 2 slices
per person on top of the pilaf.

SERVES 6

Preparation time 10 minutes
Cooking time 1 hour 10 minutes

INGREDIENTS

1	2 × 400 g (13 oz) cans chopped tomatoes
2	2 tablespoon chopped basil
3	2 aubergines
4	250 g (8 oz) soft goats' cheese, sliced or crumbled
5	50 g (2 oz) Parmesan cheese, freshly grated

STORE CUPBOARD

spray oil, for oiling; 2 large garlic cloves, crushed; 4 tablespoons extra virgin olive oil; 1 teaspoon caster sugar; salt and black pepper

Aubergine & Goats' Cheese Gratin

■ Lightly oil a 1.5 litre (2½ pint) baking dish with spray oil. Put the tomatoes, garlic, half the oil, sugar, basil and salt and pepper in a saucepan and bring to the boil.

■ Reduce the heat and simmer for about 30 minutes until reduced and thickened.

■ Cut each aubergine lengthways into 6 thin slices. Season the remaining oil with salt and pepper, then brush the aubergine slices with the seasoned oil.

■ Cook under a preheated hot grill for 3–4 minutes on each side until charred and tender.

■ Arrange one-third of the aubergine slices, overlapping them slightly, in the base of the prepared dish. Add one-third of the tomato sauce and one-third of the goats' cheese and Parmesan. Repeat these layers, finishing with the 2 cheeses.

■ Bake in a preheated oven, 200°C (400°F), Gas Mark 6, for 30 minutes until bubbling and golden.

Preparation time 20 minutes
Cooking time 35 minutes

INGREDIENTS

1 250 g (8 oz) Camargue red rice

2 750 g (1½ lb) pumpkin, peeled, deseeded and diced

3 5 tablespoons finely chopped fresh basil, plus extra leaves to garnish

4 50 g (2 oz) Parmesan cheese, coarsely grated, plus shavings to garnish

STORE CUPBOARD

1 litre (1¾ pints) vegetable stock; 1 tablespoon olive oil; 1 onion, finely chopped; 2 garlic cloves, finely chopped; salt and black pepper

Red Rice & Pumpkin Risotto

■ Put the stock in a large saucepan, add the rice and simmer for 35 minutes.

■ Meanwhile, heat the oil in a frying pan, add the onion and cook, stirring occasionally, for 5 minutes or until softened. Add the garlic, pumpkin and a little salt and pepper, mix together, then cover and cook over moderate heat for 10 minutes, stirring occasionally.

■ Drain the rice and reserve the cooking liquid. Stir the chopped basil into the frying pan with the drained rice and grated Parmesan. Adjust the seasoning and moisten with the reserved rice liquid if necessary.

■ Spoon into shallow dishes and serve garnished with extra basil leaves and Parmesan shavings.

Preparation time 15 minutes
Cooking time 30–40 minutes

INGREDIENTS

1	**300 g (10 oz) fresh root ginger, peeled, finely shredded**
2	**500 g (1 lb) firm bean curd (tofu), drained, cut into 1 cm (½ inch) cubes**
3	**2 tablespoons light soy sauce**
4	**3 tablespoons ready-made tamarind paste or 2 tablespoons lime juice**
5	**small handful of coriander leaves, to garnish**

STORECUPBOARD

sunflower oil, for deep-frying; 2 garlic cloves, finely chopped; 40 g (1½ oz) coconut, palm or brown sugar; 2 tablespoons vegetable stock

Sweet & Sour Ginger Bean Curd

■ Heat 5 cm (2 inches) of oil in a wok over a medium heat. Deep-fry all the ginger without stirring for 2–3 minutes. Move the ginger with a slotted spoon until golden brown, then drain on kitchen paper.

■ Lower the bean curd cubes into the oil, in batches, and deep-fry for 5–6 minutes until lightly browned and soft inside. Drain on kitchen paper.

■ Remove most of the oil, leaving 1½ tablespoons in the wok. Stir-fry the garlic over a medium heat for 1–2 minutes or until lightly browned. Add the sugar, soy sauce, stock or water and tamarind purée or lime juice and stir on a low heat until slightly thickened. Taste and adjust the seasoning. Add the bean curd and most of the crispy ginger and mix together.

■ Spoon into 4 warm serving bowls and garnish with the remainder of the crispy ginger.

DESSERTS

Preparation time 10 minutes
Cooking time 12–15 minutes

INGREDIENTS

1   4 egg yolks

2   150 ml (1¼ pint) cream sherry

3   large pinch of ground cinnamon

4   425 g (14 oz) can black cherries in syrup

5   2 amaretti biscuits, crumbled, to decorate

STORE CUPBOARD

125 g (4 oz) caster sugar

Cherry & Cinnamon Zabaglione

■ Pour 5 cm (2 inches) of water into a medium saucepan and bring to the boil. Cover with a large heatproof bowl, making sure that the water does not touch the base of the bowl. Reduce the heat so that the water is simmering, then add the egg yolks, sugar, sherry and cinnamon to the bowl. Whisk for 5–8 minutes until very thick and foamy, and the custard leaves a trail when the whisk is lifted above the mixture.

■ Drain off some of the cherry syrup and then tip the cherries and just a little of the syrup into a small saucepan. Warm through, then spoon into 4 dessert glasses.

■ Pour the warm zabaglione over the top and decorate with the amaretti biscuits. Serve immediately.

SERVES 4

Preparation time 10 minutes
Cooking time 7–8 minutes

INGREDIENTS

1	40 g (1½ oz) unsalted butter
2	3 dessert apples, cored and thickly sliced
3	2 large pinches ground cinnamon
4	4 ready-made pancakes, about 20 cm (8 inches) in diameter
5	4 tablespoons chocolate and hazelnut spread

STORE CUPBOARD

icing sugar, for dusting

Chocolate Apple Pancakes

■ Melt half the butter in a large frying pan, then add the apple slices and fry for 3–4 minutes, stirring and turning until hot and lightly browned. Sprinkle with cinnamon.

■ Separate the pancakes, then spread with chocolate spread. Divide the apples among the pancakes, spooning them on to cover half of each pancake. Fold the uncovered sides over the apples.

■ Heat the remaining butter in the frying pan, add the pancakes and fry for a couple of minutes on each side to warm the pancakes through. Transfer to shallow plates and dust with sifted icing sugar.

TRY IT WITH PEACHES

For peach melba pancakes, fry
2 large, thickly sliced peaches in
the butter instead of the apples,
omitting the cinnamon. Spread
the pancakes with 4 tablespoons
raspberry jam, then add the peaches
and fold. Warm through, then serve
sprinkled with fresh raspberries, a
dusting of icing sugar and a scoop
of ice cream.

SERVES 4

Preparation time 15 minutes, plus freezing

INGREDIENTS

1	1 large ripe Charentais or Galia melon, chilled
2	1 tablespoon peeled and finely grated fresh root ginger
3	juice of 2 limes

STORE CUPBOARD

150 g (5 oz) caster sugar

Melon, Ginger & Lime Sorbet

■ Cut the melon in half and remove and discard the seeds, then roughly chop the flesh – you need about 450 g (14½ oz). Place in a blender or food processor with the sugar, ginger and lime juice, then blend until smooth.

■ Transfer the sorbet to an ice cream maker and process according to the manufacturer's instructions. If you don't have an ice cream maker, place the mixture in a freezer-proof container and freeze for about 2–3 hours or until ice crystals have appeared on the surface. Beat with a hand-held electric whisk until smooth, then return to the freezer. Repeat this process twice more until you have a fine-textured sorbet and freeze until firm.

■ Remove the sorbet from the freezer about 10 minutes before serving. Serve, scooped into glasses with a wafer.

Preparation time 5 minutes, plus freezing

INGREDIENTS

1	250 g (8 oz) frozen mixed summer berries
2	75 ml (3 fl oz) spiced berry cordial
3	2 tablespoons Kirsch
4	1 tablespoon lime juice

Summer Berry Sorbet

■ Put a shallow plastic container in the freezer to chill. Process the frozen berries, cordial, Kirsch and lime juice in a food processor or blender to a smooth purée. Be careful not to over-process, as this will soften the mixture too much.

■ Spoon into the chilled container and freeze for at least 25 minutes. Spoon into serving bowls and serve.

SWITCH TO RASPBERRIES

For raspberry sorbet: replace the main recipe ingredients with 250 g (8 oz) frozen raspberries, 75 ml (3 fl oz) elderflower cordial, 2 tablespoons of crème de cassis and 1 tablespoon of lemon juice. Proceed as in the main recipe.

SERVES 8–10

Preparation time 20 minutes, plus cooling
  and chilling
Cooking time 35 minutes

INGREDIENTS

1	300 g (10 oz) good-quality plain dark chocolate with chilli (70% cocoa solids), broken into pieces
2	150 g (5 oz) unsalted butter, diced
3	6 eggs, separated
4	1 red chilli, thinly sliced
5	grated rind and juice of 1 lime

STORE CUPBOARD

125 g (4 oz) caster sugar; 100 g (3½ oz) golden caster sugar

Chocolate & Chilli Mousse Cake

■ Line the base of a 20 cm (8 inch) springform cake tin with nonstick baking paper. Melt the chocolate and butter in a heatproof bowl set over a saucepan of gently simmering water, stirring occasionally, making sure the water doesn't touch the base of the bowl.

■ Meanwhile, whisk the egg yolks with the caster sugar in a bowl with a hand-held electric whisk until pale and thick. Stir in the melted chocolate mix.

■ Whisk the egg whites in a separate large, grease-free bowl until they form soft peaks. Fold a couple of tablespoons of the egg white into the chocolate mixture to loosen, then fold in the remaining egg white with a metal spoon.

■ Pour the mixture into the prepared tin and bake in a preheated oven, 180°C (350°F), Gas Mark 4, for 20 minutes. Remove from the oven, cover with foil (to prevent a crust forming) and leave to cool. Chill in the refrigerator for at least 4 hours or overnight.

■ Make the syrup. Combine the chilli, lime rind and juice, golden caster sugar with 150 ml (¼ pint) water in a small saucepan and heat over a low heat, stirring, until the sugar has dissolved.

■ Bring to the boil, then simmer for 10 minutes until syrupy. Leave to cool. Remove the cake from the refrigerator 30 minutes before serving in slices, with the syrup poured over.

SERVES 4

Preparation time 15 minutes
Cooking time about 10 minutes

INGREDIENTS

1   **2 eggs**

2   **150 ml (¼ pint) milk**

3   **4 dessert apples, cored and thickly sliced**

4   **150 g (5 oz) frozen blackberries**

STORE CUPBOARD

125 g (4 oz) plain flour; 4 tablespoons caster sugar; sunflower oil, for deep-frying; icing sugar, for dusting

Apple Fritters with Blackberry Sauce

■ Separate one egg and put the white into one bowl and the yolk and the whole egg into a second bowl. Add the flour and half the caster sugar to the second bowl. Whisk the egg white until if forms soft peaks, then use the same whisk to beat the flour mixture until smooth, gradually whisking in the milk. Fold in the egg white.

■ Pour the oil into a deep, heavy-based saucepan until it comes one-third of the way up the side, then heat until it reaches 180–190ºC (350–375ºF), or until a cube of bread browns in 30 seconds. Dip a few apple slices in the batter and turn gently to coat. Lift out one slice at a time and lower carefully into the oil. Deep-fry, in batches, for 2–3 minutes, turning until evenly golden. Remove with a slotted spoon and drain on kitchen paper.

■ Meanwhile, put the blackberries and the remaining sugar in a small saucepan with 2 tablespoons water and heat for 2–3 minutes until hot. Arrange the fritters on serving plates, spoon the blackberry sauce around and dust with a little icing sugar.

MAKE BANANA FRITTERS

For banana fritters with raspberry sauce, use 4 thickly sliced bananas in place of the apples. Use 150 g (5 oz) of frozen raspberries instead of the blackberries. Proceed as in the main recipe.

SERVES 4

Preparation time 10 minutes
Cooking time 10–12 minutes

INGREDIENTS

1   **8 firm but ripe fresh figs**

2   **75 g (3 oz) soft goats' cheese**

3   **8 mint leaves**

4   **150 g (5 oz) baby rocket leaves**

STORE CUPBOARD

3 tablespoons extra virgin olive oil; 1 teaspoon lemon juice; salt and black pepper

Baked Figs with Goats' Cheese

■ Cut a cross in the top of each fig without cutting through the base. Put 1 teaspoonful of the goats' cheese and a mint leaf in each fig. Transfer to a roasting tin, then season with salt and pepper and drizzle with 2 tablespoons of the oil.

■ Bake in a preheated oven, 190°C (375°F), Gas Mark 5, for 10–12 minutes until the figs are soft and the cheese has melted.

■ Put the baby rocket leaves in a bowl. Whisk together the remaining oil, lemon juice, salt and pepper and drizzle over the leaves. Serve with the figs.

SERVES 4

Preparation time 10 minutes

INGREDIENTS

1	400 g (13 oz) fresh strawberries
2	4–5 lavender flower stems, plus extra to decorate
3	400 g (13 oz) Greek-style yogurt
4	4 ready-made meringue nests

STORE CUPBOARD

2 tablespoons icing sugar, plus extra for dusting

Strawberry & Lavender Crush

■ Reserve 4 small strawberries for decoration. Hull the remainder, put in a bowl with the icing sugar and mash together with a fork. Alternatively, process the strawberries and icing sugar in a food processor or blender to a smooth purée. Pull off the lavender flowers from the stems and crumble them into the purée to taste.

■ Put the yogurt in a bowl, crumble in the meringues, then lightly mix together. Add the strawberry purée and fold together with a spoon until marbled. Spoon into 4 dessert glasses.

■ Cut the reserved strawberries in half, then use together with the lavender flowers to decorate the desserts. Lightly dust with icing sugar and serve immediately.

SERVES 4

Preparation time 5 minutes, plus chilling
Cooking time 3–4 minutes

INGREDIENTS

1	175 g (6 oz) plain dark chocolate, broken into pieces
2	100 ml (3 fl oz) double cream
3	3 eggs, separated
4	cocoa powder, for dusting

Rich Chocolate Mousse

■ Put the chocolate and cream in a heatproof bowl set over a saucepan of gently simmering water, making sure the water does not touch the base of the bowl, and stir until the chocolate has melted. Remove the bowl from the heat and leave the mixture to cool for 5 minutes, then beat in the egg yolks one at a time.

■ Whisk the egg whites in a separate clean bowl until stiff, then lightly fold into the chocolate mixture until combined. Spoon the mousse into 4 dessert glasses or cups and chill for 2 hours. Dust with cocoa powder before serving.

ADD A CLASSIC TWIST

For chocolate and orange mousse, follow the main recipe, but add the grated rind of 1 large orange and 2 tablespoons Grand Marnier to the melted chocolate and cream. Proceed as in the main recipe.

SERVES 4

Preparation time 15 minutes, plus chilling
Cooking time 30 minutes

INGREDIENTS

1	2 eggs, plus 2 extra egg yolks
2	400 ml (13 fl oz) can reduced-fat coconut milk
3	125 ml (4 fl oz) semi-skimmed milk
4	150 g (5 oz) raspberries
5	5 g (1 teaspoon) butter, for greasing

STORE CUPBOARD

125 g (4 oz) granulated sugar; 2 tablespoons caster sugar

Coconut Crème Caramel

■ Heat the granulated sugar with 125 ml (4 fl oz) water in a small saucepan, stirring occasionally, until the sugar has just dissolved. Bring to the boil and cook, without stirring, for 5 minutes until golden.

■ Take the pan off the heat, add 2 tablespoons of boiling water then stand well back, tilting the pan to mix, until the bubbles have subsided. Divide the caramel between 4 x 250 ml (9 fl oz) metal pudding moulds, then swirl the caramel over the inside. Put the moulds in a roasting tin.

■ Whisk the eggs, egg yolks and caster sugar together to mix. Pour the coconut milk and semi-skimmed milk into a saucepan and bring just to the boil, then gradually whisk into the eggs. Strain into the moulds.

■ Pour 125 ml (4 fl oz) hot (not boiling) water into the roasting tin to come halfway up the sides of the moulds. Cover the tops loosely with buttered foil then bake in a preheated oven, 160°C (325°F), Gas Mark 3, for 30 minutes until just set. Remove from the oven and leave the moulds in the water for 10 minutes. Lift them out, allow to cool then chill for 4 hours or longer until required.

■ When ready to serve, dip the bases of the moulds into boiling water for 10 seconds, loosen, then turn out on to rimmed serving plates. Decorate with raspberries.

MAKE IT CHOCOLATEY

For chocolate custard pots, whisk 2 eggs, 2 egg yolks and 50 g (2 oz) caster sugar together. Heat 150 ml (¼ pint) double cream and 450 ml (¾ pint) milk in a pan with 150 g (5 oz) dark chocolate, stirring until melted. Whisk into the eggs then pour into small heatproof dishes. Cook as in the main recipe for 20–25 minutes. Cool and serve with cream.

Preparation time 5 minutes
Cooking time 8–10 minutes

INGREDIENTS

1	4 bananas, unpeeled
2	8 tablespoons fat-free Greek yogurt
3	4 tablespoons oatmeal or fine porridge oats
4	125 g (4 oz) blueberries
5	runny honey, to serve

Griddled Bananas with Blueberries

■ Heat a ridged griddle pan over a medium-hot heat, add the bananas and griddle for 8–10 minutes, or until the skins are beginning to blacken, turning occasionally.

■ Transfer the bananas to serving dishes and, using a sharp knife, cut open lengthways.

■ Spoon over the yogurt and sprinkle with the oatmeal or oats and blueberries. Serve immediately, drizzled with a little honey.

MAKE A YOGURT

For oatmeal, ginger and sultana
yogurt, mix ½ teaspoon ground
ginger with 115 g (4 oz) yogurt in a
bowl. Sprinkle with 2–4 tablespoons
soft dark brown sugar, according
to taste, the oatmeal and 45 g
(1½ oz) sultanas. Leave to stand
for 5 minutes before serving.

SERVES 8

Preparation time 35 minutes, plus cooling
Cooking time 25 minutes

INGREDIENTS

1	4 egg whites
2	1 teaspoon cornflour
3	200 g (7 oz) ready-to-eat dried apricots
4	150 ml (¼ pint) double cream
5	150 g (5 oz) fromage frais

STORE CUPBOARD

250 g (8 oz) caster sugar, plus extra for sprinkling; 1 teaspoon white wine vinegar

Apricot Meringue Swirl

■ Whisk the egg whites until stiff peaks form. Gradually whisk in the sugar, then whisk for a few minutes more until the mixture is thick and glossy.

■ Mix the cornflour and vinegar together until they are smooth. Fold into the meringue mixture.

■ Spoon into a 33 × 23 cm (13 × 9 inch) Swiss roll tin lined with nonstick baking paper snipped diagonally into the corners and standing a little above the top of the sides. Spread level. Bake in a preheated oven, 190°C (375°F), Gas Mark 5, for 10 minutes until biscuit-coloured and well risen. Reduce the heat to 160°C (325°F), Gas Mark 3, for 5 minutes until just firm to the touch and the top is slightly cracked.

■ Cover a clean tea towel with nonstick baking paper and sprinkle with a little sugar. Turn the hot meringue out on to the paper, remove the tin and leave to cool for 1–2 hours. Meanwhile, simmer the apricots in 300 ml (½ pint) water for 10 minutes until tender. Cool, then purée until smooth.

■ Peel the lining paper off the meringue when ready to serve, then spread with the apricot purée. Whip the cream until it forms soft swirls, then fold in the fromage frais and spoon over the apricot purée.

■ Roll up the meringue to make a log shape, starting from a short side and using the paper to help. Transfer to a serving plate and cut into thick slices to serve.

TRY DIFFERENT FRUIT

For kiwi and passion fruit swirl,
make the meringue as in the main
recipe. Fill with 300 ml (½ pint)
whipped double cream, then
sprinkle with 3 chopped kiwi fruits
and the seeds from 3 passion fruits.

Preparation time 15 minutes, plus cooling and chilling

INGREDIENTS

1	150 g (5 oz) good-quality milk chocolate, broken into pieces
2	200 g (7 oz) canned caramel
3	250 ml (8 fl oz) double cream
4	40 g (1½ oz) bar milk chocolate with golden honeycomb, roughly chopped, plus extra to decorate

Caramel & Honeycomb Mousse

■ Melt the chocolate in a heatproof bowl set over a saucepan of gently simmering water, stirring occasionally, making sure that the water doesn't touch the base of the bowl. Leave to cool slightly.

■ Place the caramel in a bowl with the cream and whisk with a hand-held electric whisk until the mixture starts to thicken and leaves a trail.

■ Stir a little of the caramel mixture into the melted chocolate, then fold the chocolate mixture into the caramel mixture until well combined. Stir in the chocolate honeycomb.

■ Spoon into 6 small glasses and chill for 15–30 minutes (no longer, otherwise the honeycomb will start to dissolve). Decorate with a little extra chocolate honeycomb before serving.

SERVES 6

Preparation time 20 minutes, plus cooling
   and freezing
Cooking time 4 minutes

INGREDIENTS

 25 g (1 oz) fresh mint, plus a few sprigs
to decorate

STORE CUPBOARD

200 g (7 oz) caster sugar; pared rind and juice
of 3 lemons; icing sugar, to dust

Mint Granita

■ Put the caster sugar and 300 ml
(½ pint) water into a saucepan, add the
lemon rind and gently heat until the sugar
has dissolved. Increase the heat and boil
for 2 minutes.

■ Tear the tips off the mint stems and
finely chop to give about 3 tablespoons,
then reserve. Add the larger mint leaves
and stems to the hot syrup and leave
for 1 hour to cool and for the flavours
to develop.

■ Strain the syrup into a jug, add the
chopped mint and top up to 600 ml
(1 pint) with extra cold water. Pour into
a small roasting tin and freeze the mixture
for 2–3 hours or until mushy.

■ Break up the ice crystals with a fork,
then return to the freezer for 2–3 more
hours, breaking up with a fork once or
twice until the mixture is the consistency
of crushed ice. Serve now, spooned into
small glass tumblers, decorated with tiny
sprigs of mint dusted with icing sugar,
or leave in the freezer until required.

■ If leaving in the freezer, allow to soften
for 15 minutes before serving. If frozen
overnight or longer, break up with a fork
before serving.

INDEX

PICTURE CREDITS

Octopus Publishing Group 7, 29, 33, 165, 185, 189; Frank Adam
59; Stephen Conroy 9, 47, 69, 81, 83, 85, 91, 97, 113, 119, 131, 149;
Will Heap 8, 37, 99, 103, 115, 139, 147; William Lingwood 27, 53,
75, 121, 145, 157, 163, 173, 177; David Loftus 125; Lis Parsons 39,
45, 49, 60-61, 65, 73, 77, 87, 89, 132-133, 153; William Reavell
35, 109, 111; William Shaw 20-21, 25, 51, 55, 57, 71, 79, 117, 123,
135, 137, 141, 142, 160-161, 167, 171, 181, 183, 187; Eleanor Skan 159;
Simon Smith 23, 43; Ian Wallace 5, 6, 31, 41, 63, 67, 93, 95,
100-101, 105, 107, 127, 129, 151, 155, 169, 175, 179.